20 Bicycle Tours in the Finger Lakes

20 Bicycle Tours in the Finger Lakes

Second Edition

Mark Roth and Sally Walters

Photographs by the Authors

Backcountry Publications, Inc.   Woodstock, Vermont

To Rose Roth, Sam Roth, Anne Walters, and to the memory of Oliver P. Walters.

An Invitation to the Reader—Although it is unlikely that the roads you cycle on these tours will change much with time, some road signs, landmarks, and other items may. If you find that changes have occurred on these routes, please let us know so we may correct them in future editions. The authors and publisher also welcome other comments and suggestions. Address all correspondence:

Editor, *Bicycle Tours*
Backcountry Publications, Inc.
P.O. Box 175
Woodstock, Vermont 05091

© 1983, 1987 by Mark Roth and Sally Walters
All rights reserved
Second edition, Third printing: Updated 1992
Published by Backcountry Publications, Inc.
A division of The Countryman Press, Inc.
Woodstock, Vermont 05091
Printed in the United States of America
Photographs by the authors
Design and maps by Richard Widhu

Library of Congress Cataloging-in-Publication Data

Roth, Mark.
    20 bicycle tours in the Finger Lakes.

    Bibliography: p. 158
    1. Bicycle touring—New York (State)—Finger
Lakes Region—Guide-books. 2. Finger Lakes Region (N.Y.)
—Description and travel—Guide-books.   I. Walters, Sally.
II. Title. III. Title: Twenty bicycle tours in the
Finger Lakes.
GV1045.5.N72F567   1987   917.47'8   87-1004
ISBN 0-942440-39-0

Acknowledgments

For their assistance in making our travels more enjoyable or our research more complete, we would like to thank Clare Bavis, Noreen Black, Bruce Gilman, Richard Hubbard, Henry Maus, Robert Moody, Winnie Peer, Marjory Allen Perez, Marvin Rapp, Betsy and David Schlesinger, Teresa Thurn, William and Robert Vierhile, Pat Vitalone, and Marian and John Winkelman. We are also grateful for the help given by the directors and staffs of area historical societies and museums, particularly those of the Cayuga Museum of History and Art, the Geneva Historical Society, the Livingston County Historical Society, the Ontario County Historical Society, and the Yates County Historical Society. Most of all, our appreciation goes to editor Susan Edwards, especially for her enthusiasm and fine sense of style.

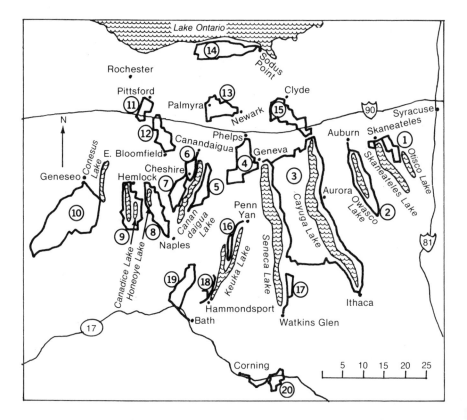

Contents

Introduction

What's special about New York's Finger Lakes region? The narrow, finger-shaped lakes themselves are surely the primary attraction. There are similar groups of lakes in the world—in the Yukon, Chile, Sweden, and New Zealand—but none closer than an expensive plane ride away. Other outstanding natural features include the highest waterfalls east of the Rockies, cascades, glens, and the Genesee River Gorge. The area is small and topography changes quickly, so cycling is never monotonous.

The major wine-making region in the eastern United States is in the Finger Lakes; about three dozen wineries welcome visitors for tours or tastings. Vineyards scale seemingly impossible slopes, highlighting pleasingly varied pastoral scenes—from fields of small buckwheat plants to acres of golden sunflowers. Lakes and hills, farms and colleges, forests and fields, cities and hamlets—all can be visited in a day of leisurely cycling, with time out for a swim.

Two of the Finger Lakes are very long, but the other nine are from three to sixteen miles; a car can pass them by in minutes, yet they can be your companions for days of cycling. On a bike you can smell the spring sweetness of fruit blossoms and the fall ripeness of grapes, hear the goldfinches, or feel the temperature drop as you approach one of the deep, cool lakes on a summer day. Enhancing the delight of cycling here is an extensive network of paved, well-maintained back roads with very light traffic. (When asked about the seemingly endless miles of roads serving only scattered farms, a young farmer smiled, "You'd be surprised," he said, "how many farmers are town road supervisors.")

Most cyclists' moods change: sometimes we pedal quickly, exhilarated with pure motion; sometimes we stop and putter—swim, explore a path or museum, or pick wild berries. You can use the maps and route directions to ride fast on uncrowded, scenic roads; or you can take your time, reading our background paragraphs to learn a bit about the history, geology, architecture, and personalities of the Finger Lakes. This book is intended for all moods.

The Terrain

The eleven bodies of water that give the Finger Lakes region its name and special character range from three-mile-long Canadice to forty-mile Cayuga. In general, the northern part of the area is rather level, with many places of culture or historical interest in and around such small cities as Auburn, Seneca Falls, Geneva, and Canandaigua. The southern ends of the lakes are tucked between high hills; towns are fewer and smaller, the scenery is more spectacular, and cycling is more strenuous.

The land between the lakes is characterized by forested rolling hills and farmed valleys. The field mosaic includes pasture for dairy herds, vineyards, orchards, and hay, wheat, oats, rye, beans, tomatoes and other vegetables. Maximum relief is seldom over 1,000 feet—the highest point is Gannett Hill (2,256'), west of Canandaigua Lake. Since the hills and lakes trend north-south, riding in these directions is usually easier than riding east-west.

Greatly simplified, and skipping an odd few million years here and there, the Finger Lakes came about something like this: Thousands of feet of sedimentary rock (mostly limestone, sandstone, and shale) formed under a shallow inland sea. The land rose, sank, rose again, was worn down and dissected by streams. Then, during the Ice Age, two separate glacial advances deepened and widened the already existing north-south stream valleys, forming the beds of the present lakes. Some of the gouging was extraordinarily powerful—the bottom of Seneca Lake, for example, is almost 200 feet below sea level. East-west streams were not deepened so much; left high above the new valley floors, but not dry, they form the many waterfalls and glens for which the area is known. The final gift of the glaciers was the Valley Heads Moraine, hills of glacial debris, damming the lakes to the south.

Of the Finger Lakes climate an eighteenth-century traveler wrote: "No part of America is better suited for dairy farms; for at no time is the weather so hot but butter can be made and preserved." May through September is the prime cycling season, though April always has some perfect days, and comfortable weather continues through October, with fall colors peaking about the middle of that month. Rain is distributed evenly through the warmer months, and high temperatures seldom exceed 90°F. Cities can absorb considerable heat, but in the countryside cool nights are the rule.

The Tours

The tours described here range from a few level miles to a 115-mile ride, though most are between 25 and 40 miles. All end where they begin. Some rides are along lake shores, offering chances to swim or fish; others climb high ridges between the lakes, with panoramic views. You can ride through orchards and pick apples, or by vineyards and visit wineries. (The Finger Lakes is the oldest commercial winemaking area in the United States, today second only to California in production.) You can choose rural rides where the only evidence you'll see of man is as farmer or logger, or tours that can include visits to historic buildings, museums, antique shops, crafts fairs, colleges and universities.

In selecting a tour, the first criterion is probably length. Next, you might consider the characterization of the cycling: easy, moderate, strenuous. This judgment is based primarily on the height and steepness of hills to be climbed, but it isn't only hills that make cycling difficult. The road surface quality counts for a lot, and the direction and strength of the wind is even more important. The introductory paragraphs before each tour give a quick preview of what that tour offers. If a tour seems appealing, read on.

It is best to read to the end of a tour before you begin, to know whether to bring food, a bathing suit, or other special equipment. At intersections, continue straight unless a turn is indicated. Sometimes a direction to continue straight is given, and sometimes not, depending on the likelihood of confusion and the distance from the last turn. To avoid compounding errors and to eliminate the need for a cyclometer, calculate your mileage from one point to the next, rather than from the start of the tour. Signposting can change (signs are swept away by snow plowing each winter), but you should find roads where we describe them. Since more roads are paved each year, you may occasionally find a paved road where our directions indicate a gravel one. Road names and numbers at

The southern Finger Lakes region abounds in waterfalls; this one is in Fillmore Glen State Park.

unsignposted corners are given so that when you come upon a sign farther along you can confirm your position.

Lunch or mid-tour rest stops are often suggested, and occasionally restaurants near a tour's finish are mentioned. Overnight accommodations are detailed for the multi-day tours; elsewhere lodgings are suggested when they are of particular interest. Cyclists may be especially interested in bed and breakfast places which have sprung up in recent years. Brochures listing many of the bed and breakfasts and small inns can be obtained from the Finger Lakes Association, 309 Lake Street, Penn Yan, NY 14527 (315-536-7488 or 800-548-4386) and from the Finger Lakes Bed and Breakfast Association, P.O. Box 6576, Ithaca, NY 14851.

Maps

Ordinary oil company maps of New York State are sufficient for finding the starting points of these tours. For cycling, the best maps to supplement ones printed here are produced by each county's highway department. These can be obtained by writing to the addresses given at the end of this book. The United States Geological Survey produces excellent maps, but the scales covering the Finger Lakes fall between the chairs: The 1:24,000 or 7½' series (1" equals 2,000') has great detail but requires almost 100 sheets to cover the area; while the 1:250,000 series covers the region in only two sheets but does not show most of the small roads used on these tours. These two sheets of the latter series (the Elmira and Rochester quadrangles) are invaluable, however, for getting an overall picture of the terrain. Maps can be ordered from the United States Geological Survey, Map Distribution Branch, Box 25286, Denver Federal Center, Denver, CO 80225. Maps intended for cyclists are available free from the Finger Lakes State Commission, R.D. #3, Trumansburg, NY 14886. Again, these maps do not show all the small back roads, but do give a good overview.

Bicycling Safety and Equipment

Whenever possible, tours follow quiet country roads or highways with shoulders. Still, following a described tour or being on a bike route is no guarantee of safety. Alertness and good judgment are always needed—even on little-used farm roads. Backcountry residents can get used to driving rather fast on their own roads; from experience they expect little traffic, and may be ill-prepared to encounter cyclists.

Common sense should govern riding behavior. Keeping to the right with the traffic, signaling turns, and obeying other traffic regulations is required by law. And remember the old joke about the 500-pound pet gorilla who gets to sit anywhere he pleases; a 3,000-pound motor vehicle is not going to be pushed around by a thirty-pound bicycle. So ride accordingly.

For short and easy tours, any bike will do. Covering longer distances or hilly terrain is less difficult on a lightweight bike with a choice of gears, ten being the most common number. Better made, lighter bikes increase efficiency and speed; they tackle hills more easily, and they generally have better brakes for safer descents. If you're unsure of your brakes, or any other bike part, and are uninclined to tinker, have your bike checked by a competent mechanic.

Cyclists who venture beyond convenient walking distance from assistance ought at least to be able to repair a flat tire. And carry a pump! Clear instructions for basic repairs are given in the books by Sloane and Ballantine listed under Additional Reading at the end of this book. Bike parts or assistance may be found at the bike shops listed at the end of each tour. It's wise to call first, to be sure the shop is open and has the parts or skills you need.

1

Skaneateles

25 miles; moderate to easy cycling
Rolling hills with gradual inclines
County map: Onondaga

The village of Skaneateles, the "Eastern Gateway to the Finger Lakes," makes as pleasant an introduction to the region as one could wish. Its quaint main street curves around the north end of the lake that William Seward, Lincoln's Secretary of State, called "the most beautiful body of water in the world." The village has excellent eating places, an historic inn, a lakefront enhanced by two landscaped parks, and the most impressive array of nineteenth-century houses and estates in the region.

The cycling route makes a figure-eight pattern; a morning loop through farmland to the east, a lunch break in Skaneateles, then a short loop through the country of the horsy set, passing the polo grounds where matches are played on Sunday afternoons in summer. You'll ride beside the two easternmost Finger Lakes, Otisco and Skaneateles, and get panoramic views from the high ridge between them. Fishing is possible in either lake, while swimming is most convenient in Skaneateles.

The tour starts in front of the Sherwood Inn in Skaneateles.

0.0   From the Sherwood Inn, ride east (with the lake to your right) on Genesee Street, Route 20.

The present Sherwood Inn traces its origin to an 1807 building used to feed and lodge passengers traveling on Isaac Sherwood's stagecoach line. It was a colorful era of fast horses and faster profits; in one year Sherwood took in over $60,000 just for carrying the mail.

It is easy to wax romantic imagining the old days of sleek four-horse teams, daring drivers and blaring horns, country inns with brass and candles and venison steak.

Thurlow Weed, who traveled the Genesee Road in 1824, adds details often overlooked. "In country inns, a traveler who objected to a stranger as a bedfellow was regarded as unreasonably fastidious. Nothing was more common, after a passenger had retired, than to be awakened by the landlord, who appeared with a tallow candle, showing a stranger into your bed."

Skaneateles has many restaurants, from world famous and expensive, to luncheonettes. Groceries are easily obtained, but are perhaps superfluous, as the twenty-mile morning loop can bring you back to town before lunch time.

0.5 Turn LEFT onto Onondaga Street, which is called New Seneca Turnpike outside the village.

In 1800 the state legislature chartered the Seneca Road and Turnpike Company to build and maintain a road from the home of John House in Utica to the courthouse in Canandaigua, over the route of the old Genesee Road. Tollgates, some with pikes to turn, were every ten miles; a two-horse wagon paid twelve and a half cents. Any wagon with wheels over twelve inches wide traveled free; it functioned as a roller-compactor for the roadway, while narrow, faster wheels cut ruts. Isaac Sherwood placed his inn near the junction of the two main east-west roads across the state, the Seneca and Cherry Valley Turnpikes.

3.0 Turn RIGHT onto Rickard Road.

3.6 At the Stop sign, cross Route 175; then immediately turn LEFT onto Masters Road.

4.8 Continue STRAIGHT at the Stop sign, crossing Bishop Hill Road; in fifty yards turn RIGHT onto Williams Road.

6.2 Go STRAIGHT at the Stop sign across Route 20, to continue south on Route 174.

8.4 Turn RIGHT, following Route 174 South and signs to Skaneateles and Borodino.

For a closer look at Otisco Lake, you can delay turning right here and ride farther on the road to the left, which gives access to Otisco's east side. The area just past the dam is popular with fishermen.

11.5 After staying on Route 174 as it climbs and turns west, away from Otisco, continue STRAIGHT at the Stop sign onto Eibert Road.

Growing wild in abandoned fields and hedgerows here-

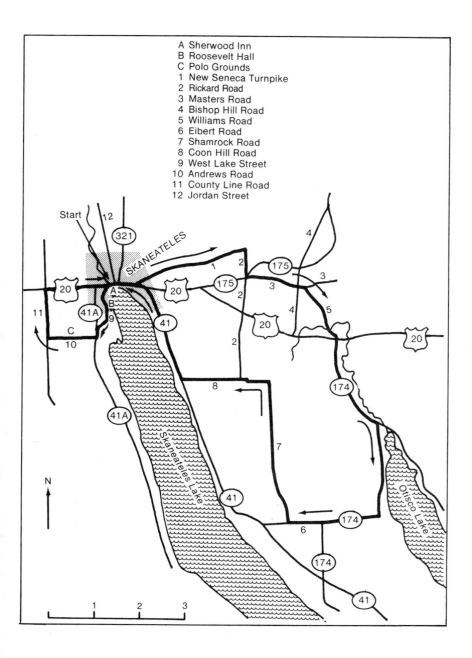

A Sherwood Inn
B Roosevelt Hall
C Polo Grounds
1 New Seneca Turnpike
2 Rickard Road
3 Masters Road
4 Bishop Hill Road
5 Williams Road
6 Eibert Road
7 Shamrock Road
8 Coon Hill Road
9 West Lake Street
10 Andrews Road
11 County Line Road
12 Jordan Street

about you may see a tall thistle-like plant with a two- to three-inch spiky head called teasel. Now considered a weed, from 1835 until early in this century teasel was a lucrative crop for area farmers. The teasel was used to raise the nap on wool cloth. Today manufacturers use wire brushes, even though they are said to do an inferior job. Skaneateles was once the world center of teasel production, with six factories and over 500 acres supplying the market. While cultivation continues in Europe, the last commercial crop was harvested here in 1956.

12.3 Turn RIGHT onto Shamrock Road.

15.3 Turn LEFT at the Stop sign onto Coon Hill Road.

17.4 After a long downhill, turn RIGHT at the Stop sign onto Route 41 North (unsignposted).

19.5 Turn LEFT at the traffic light onto East Genesee Street, Route 20 West.

On the left, the Stella Maris retreat house was once owned by the Smiths who founded the Smith-Corona typewriter company.

20.4 After passing Skaneateles' center, turn LEFT onto West Lake Street.

Lunch in Skaneateles can range from groceries alfresco in a lakeside park to a gourmet meal at the Sherwood Inn, where the fare would astound old Isaac's patrons, accustomed to "salt meat" for dinner and "for supper still more salt meat and coffee." Monday through Saturday the Sherwood serves lunch 11:30 a.m. to 4:00 p.m.; on Sunday brunch extends to 2:00 p.m. Casually dressed cyclists can enjoy the regular luncheon menu in the tavern.

With its back to the Skaneateles Lake outlet, the Old Stone Mill restaurant occupies the handsome limestone building in which the Talcot Milling Company ground flour from 1842 to 1969. The outlet was once lined with factories and mills; almost a dozen distilleries converted local grains to more easily transported whiskey. These businesses were served, as were tourists, by what was perhaps the shortest railroad in America, a five-mile line which ended in front of the Talcot Mill.

The houses along West Lake Street, representing a variety of architectural styles, form perhaps the best line-up of large old houses in the Finger Lakes. The center-piece is the white Greek Revival mansion known as

Roosevelt Hall. Built in 1839, and once owned by Samuel Montgomery Roosevelt, a cousin of Theodore's, the house now belongs to the Christian Brothers Order.

21.5 Past the country club, turn LEFT at the Stop sign onto Route 41A (unsignposted), and in 100 yards turn RIGHT onto Andrews Road, following a sign to the polo grounds.

In a couple of hundred yards you'll see the bright green of the polo grounds to your right. Matches are played every Sunday afternoon in July and August at 3:00; admission is $2.00 per car, with no charge for bikes. Once considered good exercise and training for battle, this ancient and exotic game is played on a field 300 yards long, covering the area of nine football fields. The informal setting lets you get so close you can hear horses snort, and the crack of mallets striking the wooden ball. An announcer gives a useful introduction to the sport and play-by-play commentary.

22.6 Turn RIGHT at the Stop sign onto County Line Road.

23.7 Turn RIGHT at the Stop sign onto Route 20 East (unsignposted).

Polo is played each Sunday afternoon at 3:00 at Skaneateles.

25.1 A fast downhill will soon bring you back to the village of Skaneateles.

You can swim in the purest lake water in the state (Syracuse residents drink it) at Clift Park, directly across from the Sherwood Inn; a $1.00 fee is charged.

The inn has sixteen guest rooms, decorated in various nineteenth-century styles, with rates from $45 to $70, including Continental breakfast. Excellent dinners, chosen from a largely Continental menu and a long wine list, are served in four dining rooms, all carefully furnished in Colonial style.

Many people who won't even try to pronounce Skaneateles (on local tongues it sounds like Skinny-atlas), know its famous restaurant, Krebs. It's been here since 1899, and has had many famous guests. Family-style dinners are served daily from 6:00 p.m., and a brunch is served on Sunday.

Skaneateles may remind sailing enthusiasts of the Lightning Class boat, which was developed on its lake. Sailing for pleasure and sport are very popular; it's a good guess that Skaneateles has more races and regattas than any other Finger Lake.

The most graceful time for lake travel was the steamboat era, roughly from the Civil War to World War I. Rail transportation--with dining cars--brought vacationers and wealthy cottagers to the shore of the Indians' "Long Water," and waiting boats. Successors to those steamboats are operated today by Mid-Lakes Navigation. At 10:00 a.m. Monday through Saturday a boat leaves on one of the few remaining water-borne U.S. mail delivery routes. The mailboat serves cottagers around the lake who wait on docks to snatch their mail from a long-handled fishing net. The kids at a summer camp down the lake are less passive—they usually paddle out in canoes. The mail cruise takes about three hours. For reservations, or information about other cruises, call 315-685-8500.

Bicycle shops
M & R Sports, 286 Clark Street, Auburn, NY (315-252-9069)
Nolan's Sporting Goods, 41 Genesee Street, Auburn, NY (315-252-7249)

2

Owasco Lake

38 miles; easy to moderate cycling
Some level riding with gradual hills
County map: Cayuga

A day spent circling Owasco Lake can make one believe that the lake was created especially for cyclists. Eleven-mile-long Owasco, shortest of the six major Finger Lakes, provides a sparkling backdrop throughout most of your day, yet it is short enough to leave you time to enjoy the beautiful parks at the lake's either end. Both Fillmore Glen State Park, south of the lake, and Emerson Park at its foot have excellent swimming and picknicking facilities. The state park has secluded hiking trails and rural camping, while amenities at the county-run park near the city of Auburn include a theater, museums, and a dance pavilion. Ideal as well are the roads on either side of the lake, which gently lift you above the lake and then pleasantly roll you back down again.

Begin this tour at the Seward House on South Street in Auburn, just south of the Genesee Street shopping area.

0.0 Go south on South Street, Route 38.

(To shorten this tour by about six miles you can start at Emerson Park, on the north end of Owasco Lake, and ride to Route 38 South from there.)

Among the many fine old houses along Auburn's historic South Street is the William H. Seward House, a beautifully maintained memorial to the city's most famous son. The original house was built in 1817 by Judge Elijah Miller; Seward was permitted to marry the judge's nineteen-year-old daughter in 1824 after he agreed to move into the Miller home. Through renovations and additions made from 1840 to 1870, the small late-Georgian residence grew into a thirty-room mansion in the "Anglo-Italian" style. During these years Seward went on to become State Senator, Governor, and finally Secretary of State under Lincoln and Johnson--when he made his name with the purchase of Alaska. Visitors to this remarkable home can inspect all three floors and see the transition from Federal home to Victorian mansion. All the furnishings belonged to the Seward family, the house's only occupants; clothing on display reveal that the most famous Seward was quite a diminutive fellow. The house is open Monday through Saturday afternoons from 1:00 to 5:00, March through December. Admission of $2.50 includes a narrated tour through sixteen rooms.

Other prominent Auburnians include William Burroughs, inventor of the adding machine, author and screenwriter Samuel Hopkins Adams, William Fargo of the Wells-Fargo Express Company, architect Julius Schweinfurth, and Theodore Willard Case, cofounder of the Twentieth Century-Fox film studio. The Greek Revival mansion where Case developed the AEO bulb, permitting the recording of sound on film, is now the Cayuga Museum of History and Art, open Tuesday through Saturday afternoons from 1:00 to 5:00, Saturday mornings from 9:00 to noon, and Sunday afternoons from 2:00 to 5:00. Next door is the attractive Schweinfurth Memorial Art Center (1981) with changing exhibits, open Tuesday through Friday noon to 5:00, Saturday 10:00 a.m. to 5:00 p.m., Sun. 1:00 to 5:00 p.m.

Auburn is well supplied with restaurants and food stores, including a Wegman Supermarket at the corner of Genesee and Osborne Streets. Halfway through the tour, the village of Moravia has a restaurant, food stores, and a take-out shop.

0.8 Turn LEFT at the traffic light onto Metcalf Drive, also called Clymer Road.

To see the one-time home of Harriet Tubman, don't turn left here but continue straight for about four-tenths of a mile; the house is on the left at 180 South Street Road. Built on land purchased from William Seward in 1857, the home was used as a refuge for slaves fleeing the south via the "underground railroad." With a fearlessness that amazed her contemporaries, Harriet, called "The Moses of her People," led more than three hundred slaves from bondage. The home can be visited by appointment only. Call 315-253-2621.

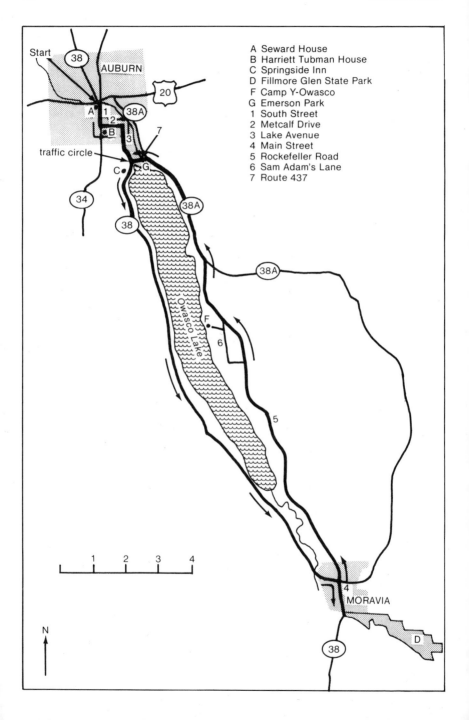

Start
38
AUBURN
20

A 1
2
38A
B
3
7

traffic circle

34

C G

38A

38

Owasco Lake

F
6

38A

5

1 2 3 4

N

4
MORAVIA

D

38

A Seward House
B Harriett Tubman House
C Springside Inn
D Fillmore Glen State Park
F Camp Y-Owasco
G Emerson Park
1 South Street
2 Metcalf Drive
3 Lake Avenue
4 Main Street
5 Rockefeller Road
6 Sam Adam's Lane
7 Route 437

1.4 Turn RIGHT at the Stop sign onto Lake Avenue.

1.8 Curve LEFT at the fork, staying on Route 38 South down the hill past the high school.

2.4 Take the second RIGHT at the traffic circle, to stay on Route 38 South.

In about a half mile you'll pass the Springside Inn, built in 1851 as a boys' boarding school. It is now a hotel-restaurant with eight guest rooms. The $55.00 for a double includes a Continental breakfast. The restaurant, known for its cheese souffle, popovers, and duck flambée, serves dinner Monday through Saturday from 5:00 to 10:00, Sunday 1:00 to 6:00. Sunday cyclists can also choose the 10:30 a.m. to 2:00 p.m. buffet brunch. A dinner theatre is offered during the summer; for reservations call 315-252-7247.

In about five miles note the fine 1835 cobblestone house on the right. Cobbles for this type of masonry were brought from the Lake Ontario plain.

By the time you reach Center Road, the gentle rise of Route 38, which has given you fine views of Owasco Lake, changes to a gradual descent. One large and several small cascades adorn the slope on your right; as you glide downhill you'll have a clear view of the lakehead marshland that is slowly encroaching on the lake.

18.1 Turn RIGHT at the Stop sign onto North Main Street.

Like Auburn, Moravia has had several notables, among them Jethro Wood, inventor of the cast iron plow, and Millard Fillmore. Fillmore's rather uneventful Presidency is commemorated in his native village by an annual bathtub race, said to be in honor of his improvements to the White House plumbing. Contestants in the late July race can either contrive their own wheeled vessel or make use of a Rent-a-Tub program.

Just off Main Street is St. Matthews Episcopal Church, whose chancel contains wood carvings by Oberammergau artist Hans Meyer.

19.2 Turn LEFT into Fillmore Glen State Park.

Near the entrance is a reconstruction of the tiny log cabin in which Millard Fillmore was born in 1800. The park's magnificent gorge was carved by Fillmore Creek, which cut its way through layers of limestone and shale, creating five waterfalls and picturesque rock formations. Eight bridges along the gorge trail cross the creek, giving exceptional views of the glen. A stream-fed swimming area has been constructed at the lower end of the gorge, with a bathhouse, pavilion, tables, and fireplaces nearby. Campsites and cabins are also available.

Leaving the park, turn right onto Route 38 North and retrace your route through the village of Moravia.

20.3 Continue STRAIGHT, north, on Main Street, which becomes Rockefeller Road after leaving the village.

Just over three miles farther is a sign marking the site of John D. Rockefeller's boyhood home. Here, Rockefeller later claimed, he raised wild turkeys for pocket money. John D.'s father, William, usually away from home dealing in patent medicines and other questionable merchandise, often returned with handsome horses and generous gifts of money for his children. Some Moravians say horse thievery was one of his sidelines, though the claim has not been proven. Indicted in 1849 for the rape of a hired girl, the father's appearances became more rare, and he soon moved his family out of the county. Today the old Rockefeller house, on private land about a mile back from the road, has decayed nearly to ground level, evidently not a relic later generations of Rockefellers were eager to preserve. Local people report the remains of a tunnel through which the elder Rockefeller was said to have escaped from a posse pursuing horse thieves.

27.1 Where Sam Adams Lane comes in from the left, you can continue STRAIGHT or make the left turn.

Both options give splendid views of the lake and well-kept farmland. Along Sam Adams Lane you'll pass the sign to Camp Y-Owasco, a lakeside recreation area that has thirty bunks in tents for American Youth Hostel members at a nominal charge. Swimming, meals, and tent camping are also available (315-784-5481).

28.7 Sam Adams Lane comes in from the left. If you have ridden it, turn LEFT at the T-junction; if not, continue STRAIGHT.

30.9 Turn LEFT at the Stop sign onto Route 38A North.

34.4 Many cyclists will want to cross to the left along this stretch, to enter Emerson Park.

One of the most entertaining and well-maintained parks in the Finger Lakes, Emerson Park has carefully tended lawns and a wide beach excellent for picnicking and

In Auburn, the Cayuga Museum of History and Art displays early cycles that make one grateful for their modern successors.

swimming; there are snack bars, an imaginative playground, and the Merry-Go-Round Playhouse, presenting musicals and comedies throughout the summer (315-255-1785). An open air museum on the site of a former Indian settlement recreates a village of the Owasco Indian culture as it would have appeared about A.D. 1100. Open in July and August, the village charges $.50 for adults, half price for children.

Across from the park's main entrance is the Agricultural Museum, open every afternoon May through October from noon to 5:00. Exhibited are many products of the local farm equipment manufacturers who united to form International Harvester.

35.1 Turn LEFT at the corner of the park onto Routes 437 and 38.

35.8 Take the first RIGHT at the traffic circle, following signs for Route 38 North and the city of Auburn.

36.8 Turn LEFT at the traffic light onto Swift Street, Route 38 North.

37.4 Turn RIGHT at the traffic light onto South Street, Route 38 North.

38.0 Bearing RIGHT at the fork will take you to the Seward House, where the tour began.

Those wishing to spend the night in Auburn will find a reasonably priced TraveLodge adjacent to the Seward House. A small licensed cafe on the premises serves meals all day.

Nearby bed-and-breakfasts include:

Fay's Point Beachhouse, RD#1 Box 147A, Route 38 South, Auburn, NY (315-253-9525)

Irish Rose B & B, 102 South Street, Auburn, NY (315-255-0196)

Bicycle shops

Bicycles Today, 88 Grant Avenue, Auburn, NY (315-253-9958)

M & R Sports, 286 Clark Street, Auburn, NY (315-252-9069)

Marjax Sporting Goods, Finger Lakes Mall, Auburn, NY (315-252-7135)

Nolan's Sporting Goods, 41 Genesee Street, Auburn, NY (315-252-7249)

3

Finger Lakes Heartland:
A three-day tour

115 miles
Cycling difficulty and terrain are given for each day
County maps: Cayuga, Schuyler, Seneca, Tompkins

Seneca and Cayuga, the longest, widest, and deepest of the Finger Lakes, lie at the heart of this region. Both occupy glacier-enlarged valleys, and both have bottoms below sea level. In song, Cornell University hails its scenic location "far above Cayuga's waters"; in fact it shares this distinction with Wells and Ithaca Colleges, while above Seneca Lake sit Hobart and William Smith Colleges. All these schools can be visited on this tour, along with a winery, several museums, and the new Women's National Historical Park in Seneca Falls, birthplace of the American Women's Rights Movement. The city of Ithaca has many excellent restaurants serving the greatest variety of food in the Finger Lakes. And for rural pleasures, this route passes some of the most scenic state parks in the area.

Most riders will want to devote three days to this tour. Fast riders can cut it down to two, while those with more time may want to spend a week or so on the circuit. The days are planned for riders seeking indoor overnight accommodations (see Introduction for lodging information). The tour begins in Geneva with a long first day to Ithaca, both cities having a selection of motels and guest houses. The second day is shorter and easier, ending at Aurora where there is an excellent old inn; and the third day returns you to your starting point in Geneva in a little over 30 miles.

Campers have greater flexibility. Both lakes are well served by excellent state parks and some private campgrounds, so there is no need to keep to the daily schedules outlined below. The state parks along the route which permit camping

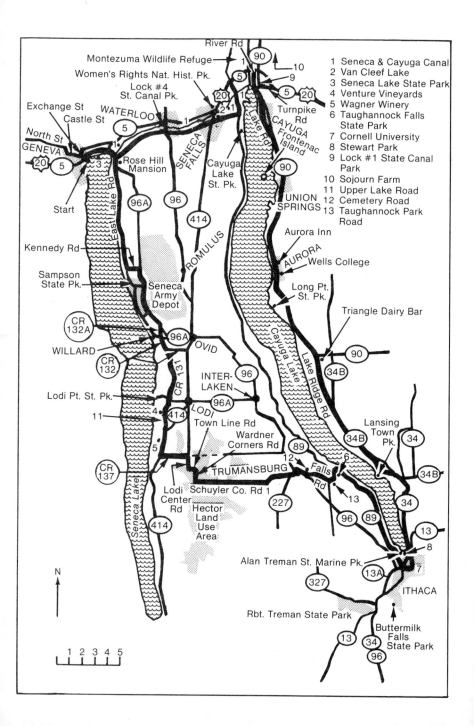

include Sampson, Taughannock Falls, Buttermilk Falls, Robert Treman, Long Point, and Cayuga Lake. Reservations for overnight stays are recommended, particularly on summer weekends. While the route is the same for campers and non-campers, riders with tents can bypass Geneva. Directions for this shortcut are given in the tour.

Day One
54 miles; moderate to strenuous cycling
Rolling terrain with one steep hill

This tour begins at the corner of Castle and Exchange Streets in Geneva's commercial district. Because there are no food sources until you reach the village of Trumansburg (forty miles from Geneva), you should bring food with you. The Geneva area is well supplied with grocery stores.

0.0 Ride south on Castle Street toward the railroad tracks and Seneca Lake. Cross the tracks and follow the highway to the RIGHT for a hundred feet. Then turn LEFT 180 degrees to follow Routes 5 and 20 East—with the lake to your right.
   The shoulder here is wide but rough. As you ride, Seneca Lake State Park, with swimming and picnicking facilities, is between the highway and the lake. The paved lakeside pathways look inviting, but unfortunately there is no exit at the park's east end.
2.1 Take the exit ramp to the RIGHT, following signs for Route 96A and Ovid and Ithaca.
   After crossing the bridge, the first right turn, onto Boody Hill's Road, leads to a good seafood restaurant, the Crow's Nest. Across an inlet from the Seneca Lake State Park Marina, the restaurant's spacious outdoor terrace and airy dining room afford pleasant marine vistas. From its dock, the fifty-passenger *Seaviewer* leaves for daily "sip-n-sail" cruises. For information or reservations call 315-781-0660.
   Soon after Boody Hill's Road you'll see Rose Hill (1839) on the left, one of the finest Greek Revival houses in the country. The mansion has been exquisitely restored, complete with the Empire furnishings popular from 1820 to 1840 (look for the characteristic claw foot). The guided tour ($2.00 for adults, $1.00 for children ten to sixteen) includes a slide show with photos of the restoration process begun

in 1965. The house is open Monday through Saturday from 10:00 a.m. to 4:00 p.m. and Sunday afternoon from 1:00 to 5:00, May through October.

3.8 Turn RIGHT onto East Lake Road.

11.3 Turn LEFT onto Kennedy Road (unsignposted). Here signs warn that continuing straight will lead to a dead end at Seneca Army Depot.

12.5 Turn RIGHT at the Stop sign onto Route 96A South.

The highway gets moderate traffic but has a wide, often paved, shoulder. To the left, behind the Army Depot fence, you may glimpse strange, specter-like members of a herd of albino deer which live on the base.

In a mile and a half you'll reach Sampson State Park. Campers may want to spend the night, or start their tour here. The park was opened by the state in 1960 on what was once the huge Sampson Naval base. During World War II, Sampson was the second-largest training facility in the country, with more than 40,000 men housed here. Forty-one of the Navy's 208 buildings remain, as well as an extensive network of roads, most now closed to motorized traffic but open to cyclists.

If you explore the park, or use its swimming or camping facilities, you may want to continue to Willard without going back to Route 96A. To do this, take the park's entrance road to the T-junction (past the circle) and turn left (south). You'll pass the maintenance garage which was once the base firehouse. Here cycle past the barrier that says *Service Road—Do Not Enter*. Thereafter, go right at all forks. You'll have an empty lakeside road all the way to the barrier marking the former boundary of the base. Beyond the barrier, the road continues along the shore, then curves left to bring you to Willard, where you rejoin the described route by turning right onto County Road 132.

17.6 Bear RIGHT at the fork, taking County Road 132A and following the sign to Willard.

17.9 Continue STRAIGHT at the Stop sign onto County Road 132. (If you chose the route through Sampson State Park, this is where you rejoin the tour.)

Willard Psychiatric Center, which has been in operation for over a century, was originally built in the early 1860s as the New York State Agricultural College. After the Civil War, Ithaca was considered a better site for the college;

there it formed the nucleus of Cornell University.

18.9 Continue STRAIGHT on County Road 131, as County Road 132 turns left.

In about four miles you'll pass a right turn for Lodi Point State Park, a secluded lakeside picnic area with bath-houses and boat-launching facilities.

23.0 Again continue STRAIGHT down the hill and past a cemetery on Upper Lake Road.

24.9 Turn RIGHT at the Yield sign onto Route 414 South (un-signposted).

In a little over a mile you'll see the octagonal building of Wagner Winery to the right. Shaded picnic tables near a small pond and the terrace of the Ginny Lee Cafe provide a picturesque setting from which to enjoy a splendid view over the vineyards to Seneca Lake. The cafe is open mid-May through mid-October 11:30 a.m. to 5:00 p.m. Monday to Saturday and from 10:00 a.m. to 5:00 p.m. on Sunday. Wagner's winery tour is followed by a generous sampling of wines. Tour times correspond to opening hours at the cafe. Wagner's production is small, and its quality is very high.

27.3 Turn LEFT onto County Road 137, and begin a stiff climb of just under two miles.

When General Sullivan's Colonial army passed this way on September 3, 1779, a soldier entered in his diary: "This day we passed over a fine Beautiful country of land adjoining Seneca Lake on the west and the Cayuga Lake on the east." The soldiers were not just sightseeing; they had been promised land once the war ended. Three years after the Sullivan campaign, the Military Tract was created; 600 acres went to privates, and more to officers. Some men settled on their land and many more sold to speculators. The township lines in the 1.5-million-acre tract were drawn with a ruler, ignoring topography. Many roads here retain the original grid pattern, forming almost mile-square boxes, representing a private's bounty. The twenty-eight townships in the tract were given classical names; on this tour you'll ride through Junius, Romulus, Ovid, Hector, Ulysses, Milton, Scipio, and Aurelius.

29.9 Turn RIGHT at the Yield sign onto Lodi Center Road (unsign-posted).

30.9 Turn LEFT at the Yield sign, onto Town Line Road. For the next 1.4 miles the surface is well-graded packed dirt and gravel.

31.3 Turn RIGHT onto Wardner Corners Road (unsignposted); it is the first right turn possible.

32.3 Turn LEFT at the Stop sign onto Schuyler County Road 1, where pavement resumes.

> You'll see signs for the Finger Lakes National Forest and its rustic Blueberry Patch Campground (see tour 17 for details). Soon you'll pass the crest of the ridge between the lakes and roll easily toward Cayuga Lake.

39.5 Turn LEFT at the Stop sign in Trumansburg onto Route 227 North.

39.9 Turn RIGHT at the Yield sign onto Route 96 South.

> When Revolutionary War soldier Abner Treman drew for his share of the military tract, he got lot #2 of township 22 (Ulysses), a strip of land three-quarters of a mile by two

Rose Hill, just east of Geneva, is considered one of the finest Greek Revival homes in the Northeast.

miles in which the village of Trumansburg is now located. The village was originally named Treman's Village; a post office error around 1814 accounts for the present spelling.

Trumansburg has a convenient supermarket and several small and good restaurants—the influence of Cornell University in nearby Ithaca is already evident. As you leave the village you'll pass a sign on your right for the Podunk Ski Center which also operates as a youth hostel. For information on this and other Finger Lakes hostels write: AYH, 459 Westcott Street, Syracuse, NY 13210.

41.0 About a quarter-mile past the school (on the right) turn LEFT onto Cemetery Road, followed by a RIGHT at the first intersection onto Falls Road. (The cemetery should be on your left.)

42.7 Turn LEFT at the Stop sign onto Taughannock Park Road; in 150 yards turn LEFT, following the sign to Taughannock Falls State Park.

Two-thirds of the way down the long hill through the park is the headquarters of the Finger Lakes State Parks Commission, where information on all the region's parks can be obtained. Also available here are the two Finger Lakes Bicycle Maps published by the Commission.

Campers may want to spend the night here, as reaching the two state parks just past Ithaca requires some uncomfortable highway riding. The park's hiking trails lead to scenic lookouts over the stream-carved gorge and 215-foot Taughannock Falls.

44.2 Turn RIGHT at the Stop sign onto Route 89 South.

Route 89 is narrow, with little or no shoulder, short sight distances, and sometimes fast traffic. It must be endured, if not enjoyed.

48.2 Turn LEFT, just before the long uphill, onto Maplewood Road.

49.2 At the Stop sign, continue STRAIGHT, to merge with Route 89 South.

53.4 After passing the Alan Treman State Marine Park and the municipal park, turn LEFT at the traffic light and cross the bridge, following signs for Route 89 and 96 South. (There is a bike path to the left of the road for about a mile before this intersection. Traffic at the bridge is very busy, and some may prefer walking across it to negotiating a left turn here.) Immediately after the bridge, take the first LEFT possible, onto

Buffalo Street (another difficult turn), and stay on this street as it curves right.

54.3 This day's ride ends at DeWitt Park, a convenient central location adjacent to Buffalo and Cayuga Streets.

The delights of Ithaca more than make up for its less-than-ideal traffic conditions. Those who choose to spend the night near town have choices ranging from the growing number of bed and breakfast establishments listed in brochures, to the sprawling Sheraton Inn complex with covered pool, spacious rooms, bar, and restaurant. Campers have a choice of Robert Treman or Buttermilk Falls State Parks, reached via busy Route 13 South. Both parks encompass spectacular glens several miles long with numerous waterfalls. They are dazzling spectacles, and convenient places to picnic or to swim in stream-fed gorge pools.

Thanks to Cornell, Ithaca is a small city with an artsy, cosmopolitan atmosphere; on and off campus, culture and natural beauty blend nicely—Ithaca well deserves its classical name. This ideal situation has only one flaw for cyclists: Just about everything in this precipitous city is up or down a very long, steep hill. Once you get up to Cornell, plan to stay there for a while. A map of the Cornell campus is available in the student union building, Willard Straight Hall, where you can also check the calendar of events. You'll find attractions from agriculture to fine arts: films, concerts, lectures, an art museum, and architectural tours of the campus (given weekly in summer). The 2,600-acre arboretum, Cornell Plantations, has miles of winding trails east of the main campus, and the well-known Laboratory of Ornithology is a couple of miles northeast, off Route 13 North, on Sapsucker Woods Road. The central campus, overlooking city and lake and bordered by two striking gorges, is perhaps the most beautiful in the country.

DeWitt Park is named for Simeon DeWitt, who laid out the townships in the military tract. Across from the park is the DeWitt Mall, small shops and restaurants in a former school. Another example of skillful urban renewal is the Ithaca Commons, a pedestrian shopping mall in the heart of the city.

Ithaca is a diner's paradise, with restaurants for every

budget and taste. Turback's, in an 1852 Victorian Gothic farmhouse near the state parks on Route 13 South, has a salad bar so complete—from breads and soup to make-your-own ice cream sundaes—that the fine entrees are almost superfluous. In the summer, area wineries offer free samples in Turback's book-lined bar. Among Ithaca's excellent vegetarian restaurants are The Cabbagetown Cafe on Eddy Street (near the Cornell campus) and the Moosewood (in the DeWitt Mall).

Day Two
27 miles; moderate cycling
Rolling terrain with one long gradual hill

There are a few grocery stores and restaurants along today's route, but it may be more convenient to stop at any of Ithaca's numerous bakeries and delis for food to carry with you.

0.0 Leave DeWitt Park by riding east on Buffalo Street (the park will be on your left); in two-tenths of a mile, turn LEFT at the second traffic light, just before the hill, onto North Aurora Street.

1.0 Turn RIGHT at the Stop sign onto East Lincoln Street; then take the first LEFT onto Lake Street. Soon you'll cross a bridge with Ithaca Falls to your right.

1.9 At the highway underpass, continue STRAIGHT, following the sign for Route 34 North.

Making the first left after the underpass will bring you to Stewart Park, featuring a small zoo, a merry-go-round, tennis courts, and picnic facilities. Fishing is allowed (swimming is not), and a concession rents canoes, row-boats, and sailboats.

The route out of Ithaca is marked by gradual uphills, with over three miles of climbing in the first seven.

7.5 Turn LEFT at the Stop sign onto Route 34B North, following the sign to King Ferry.

After this turn, past the 1830 brick tavern called Rogue's Harbor, there is a long downhill followed by a long uphill. Before the uphill, a turn to the left on Myers Road will take you to Lansing Town Park with opportunities for fishing, swimming, and picnicking. Near the turn is the Corner Cupboard Restaurant, popular for its salad bar.

15.5 Turn LEFT onto narrow Lake Ridge Road. This turn is not conspicuous; it comes after a short rise and is opposite an old cemetery.

19.7 Continue STRAIGHT at the Stop sign to join Route 90 North. The Triangle Dairy Bar at this intersection is locally popular for good, simple country fare, ice cream, and homemade desserts.

23.6 Continue STRAIGHT on Route 90, or turn LEFT onto Lake Road to visit Long Point State Park. Both routes lead to Aurora.

This peaceful boaters' park has a rustic campground; along the lake is a picnic area where a sign prohibiting swimming is generally ignored.

27.1 This day's ride ends at the Aurora Inn.

The village of Aurora was named earlier just as appealingly by the Indians, who called their settlement here Deawendote or "Village of Constant Dawn." This college town along a half-moon cove of Cayuga Lake fulfills whatever expectations its attractive names suggest. Twenty-six-year-old Henry Wells first saw Aurora in 1832 when he fetched a shipment of wheat from the old steam mill (still standing behind the Aurora Inn). In 1850 he moved to town permanently, and the same year he became president of the American Express Company, having earlier formed, with William Fargo, the famous company linking their names. Wells College, a four-year women's liberal arts school, was founded by its benefactor in 1868. Wells' large, graceful, limestone home, Glen Park (1852) is now one of the college buildings, set amid wide lawns under tall shade trees.

Under several names and serving various functions (including college dormitory), the Aurora Inn has been a village landmark since 1833. It is owned by the college (as are many of the best old buildings) and operated by a professional staff. Lunches are moderately priced and comfortable overnight accommodations cost about $45 for two, including a continental breakfast. Hotel guests are free to use college facilities which include tennis courts, a nine-hole golf course, and a lakeside swimming pier.

To explore the village further, follow the walking tour

guide for sale at Jane Morgan's Little House on Main Street.

Day Three
33.5 miles; easy to moderate cycling
Mostly level with some rolling terrain

There's a small grocery store in Aurora and opportunities to shop or dine throughout today's ride.

0.0 Leave the Aurora Inn riding north on Route 90 (the lake will be on your left).

In Oak Glen Cemetery on the north edge of the village is the grave of Henry Wells. Four miles farther, on the right, is a marker on the site of the capital of the Cayuga Indians, destroyed by Sullivan's army in 1779.

Union Springs, about six miles north of Aurora, has food stores and prepared meals. In the lake, opposite the village, is Frontenac Island, one of two islands in the Finger Lakes and the site of an early Indian burial ground that has yielded rich archeological remains.

11.1 Turn LEFT at the fork onto Lake Road.

Before construction of the Erie Canal, forty-mile-long Cayuga Lake and the extensive marshlands to its north were serious obstacles to east-west transport. The wooden Cayuga Bridge, completed in 1800 was one of the marvels of its day, spanning a mile of lake between Cayuga Village and Bridgeport. Timothy Dwight, a president of Yale, was suitably impressed when he saw it in 1804: "The bridge ... may be justly styled a stupendous erection; ... probably the longest work of the kind in the United States .... The toll is a quarter of a dollar for man and horse; the highest, I believe, in the United States." In the 1850s the bridge was allowed to deteriorate.

12.8 Continue straight through Cayuga, past the sprawling Beacon Feed Company. Go STRAIGHT at the Stop sign to rejoin Route 90 North.

14.2 Turn LEFT onto unsignposted River Road, where Turnpike Road enters from the right. In 100 feet, keep RIGHT at the fork.

You'll pass the trim park and picnic area at Lock #1 of the Cayuga and Seneca Canal, which links the lakes with the Barge Canal.

15.7 Turn LEFT onto Routes 5 and 20 West.

Shortly after crossing the canal on the bridge dedicated to French missionary Rene Menard, you'll see the entrance to the Montezuma Wildlife Refuge on your right. Details on the refuge can be found in Tour 15.

17.6 Turn LEFT at the top of the hill onto Route 89 South.

20.1 Turn RIGHT onto County Road 116 (unsignposted).

The campus of the former Eisenhower College is at this corner. If you continue south on Route 89 instead of making the right turn, you'll reach Cayuga Lake State Park in about a mile. This beautiful 186-acre park has a beach, a picnic area, pavilions, hiking trails, fourteen cabins, and nearly 300 campsites. Three miles farther south is the Locustwood Country Inn, dating from 1820. Rooms from $55 to $75 include full breakfast (315-549-7132).

County Road 116 becomes East Bayard Street at the Seneca Falls village limits. Shortly after the cemetery, Washington Street, on your right, marks the eastern boundary of the Women's Rights National Historical Park, operated by the National Park Service. If you turn right onto Washington, you'll reach the Elizabeth Cady Stanton House in two-tenths of a mile. The talented and prolific women's rights pioneer lived here with her husband and numerous children from 1847 to 1862. Van Cleef Lake, down the hill from the house, had not been created at that time; residents on this side could walk from island to island amid mills and rapids, to the village center. Tours of the restored Stanton house are conducted June through September by the Park Service.

Continuing straight on East Bayard, you'll see the Amelia Jenks Bloomer house on the right at number 53, near the junction with Washington Street. Mrs. Bloomer was active in the temperance movement, editing the society's newspaper, *The Lily*. She did not invent the costume that was named after her; Elizabeth Smith Miller, a cousin of Mrs. Stanton introduced the garment to Geneva, New York after having seen it worn by ladies in Swiss sanitariums.

22.4 Turn RIGHT at the traffic light and cross the bridge over the Cayuga and Seneca Canal. Then turn LEFT at the T-junction and continue STRAIGHT along Falls Street, Seneca Falls' main street.

At the time of the first Women's Rights Convention in

1848, Seneca Falls was a bustling mill and manufacturing town, situated along the Seneca Turnpike (now Falls Street) and a feeder canal of the Erie. When Elizabeth Cady Stanton moved here from Boston, where she had been active in the abolitionist movement, she found life in this small working class town painfully restricted. "I suffered with mental hunger," she wrote, "which, like an empty stomach, is very depressive."

Joining with four other women, some from the liberal Quaker community in nearby Waterloo, Stanton called the first Women's Rights Convention on July 19th and 20th, 1848 in the local Wesleyan Chapel. Here was drafted the radical Declaration of Sentiments and Resolutions which insisted that women "have immediate admission to all the rights and privileges which belong to them as citizens of the United States." Embellished by the speeches of well-known abolitionists Lucretia Mott and Frederick Douglass, the convention drew over three hundred people and the attention of national newspapers, which published the declaration alongside indignant editorials. Such notice added to the success of the convention, even though many supporters refused to sign the landmark document because it demanded women's suffrage.

The Park Service Visitor Center on Fall Street (open daily 9:00 a.m. to 5:00 p.m.) near the former chapel, has historical displays and information on park tours and activities. More exhibits on women's history, both local and national, are found at the Women's Hall of Fame on Fall Street, open year-round from 10:00 a.m. to 4:00 p.m. Monday through Saturday, and, from May through September, 1:00 to 4:00 p.m. on Sunday. Admission is $3.00 for adults.

The recently refurbished turn-of-the-century Gould Hotel, in the village center, has fine cuisine and a limited number of guest rooms. Standard motels are common along busy Routes 5 and 20 between here and Geneva, twelve miles west.

23.1 Turn LEFT at the traffic light onto Rumsey Street and recross the canal; in two-tenths of a mile, turn RIGHT at the Stop sign onto West Bayard Street.

In about three miles those wishing to go into Waterloo for groceries or to find lodgings in motels along Routes 5 and 20 can turn right onto Washington Street, where you'll cross the canal again and pass the canal park at Lock #4.

Two houses of the Women's Rights Park are here, those of Jane Hunt (401 East Main Street) and Mary Ann Mc-Clintock (16 East Williams Street), who helped organize the convention of 1848.

To bypass Waterloo, continue straight on West Bayard.

30.6 Turn RIGHT at the Stop sign (before the railroad tracks) onto the shoulder of Route 96A North (unsignposted). Campers headed for Sampson State Park can bypass Geneva by turning left here. You'll soon see the Rose Hill Mansion on the left, and you can pick up the tour directions at that point.

31.2 Ride to the LEFT at the fork, following signs to Geneva and Routes 5 and 20 West.

Riding these two miles of busy highway is unpleasant but unavoidable.

33.5 Turn RIGHT at the second exit to Geneva, which brings you onto Castle Street. In a block you'll be at the corner of Castle and Exchange Streets where this tour began 115 miles before.

For information on the history and sites of Geneva, see tour 4.

Bicycle shops
The Bike Rack, 414 College Street, Ithaca, NY (607-272-1010)
Black Star Bicycles, East Hill Plaza, Ithaca, NY (607-347-4117)
Geneva Bicycle Center, 493 Exchange Street, Geneva, NY (315-789-5922)
Pedal-Away, 632 West Buffalo Street, Ithaca, NY (607-272-5425)

Nearby bed and breakfasts include:
The Bay Horse B&B, 813 Ridge Road, Lansing, NY (607-533-4612)
Buttermilk Falls B&B, 110 E. Buttermilk Falls Road, Ithaca, NY (607-273-3947)
Chamberlain Mansion Inn, 30 Cayuga Street, Seneca Falls, NY (315-586-5484)
Conifer Hill B&B, 6785 Route 227, Trumansburg, NY (607-387-5849)
Front Porch, 1248 Routes 5 & 20, Waterloo, NY (315-539-8325)
Glendale Farm, 224 Bostwick Road, Ithaca, NY (607-272-8756)
Hanshaw House, 15 Sapsucker Woods Road, Ithaca, NY (607-273-8034)
James Russell Webster Inn, 115 E. Main Street, Waterloo, NY (315-539-3032)
Log Country Inn, Box 581, Ithaca, NY (607-589-4771)
Pierce House B&B, 218 S. Albany Street, Ithaca, NY (607-273-0824)
The Pillars, 9342 Route 96, Trumansburg, NY (607-387-3628)
Sage Cottage, 112 E. Main Street, Box 626, Trumansburg, NY (607-387-6449)

4

Geneva—Phelps—Gorham

37 miles; easy cycling
Level terrain with very gently rolling hills
County map: Ontario

To see rural farming landscapes that are close to kids' picture book idealizations, take a ride through Ontario County. Farmhouses are old and well kept, hedgerows and fences in good repair, woodlots healthy. More than a third of county farm income is from dairying, with the next largest amount coming from vegetable growing. The county ranks first in the nation in production of table beets and cabbage for sauerkraut, and it leads the state in wheat production. Other common crops include oats, rye, and barley; alfalfa and other hay crops; feed corn, beans, and fruits.

Places of cultural or historical interest are common on this tour, especially in and around the city of Geneva, where you start and finish. Geneva is old—the first-settled city west of Albany. Its South Main Street, laid out in 1796, has been called "the most beautiful old Colonial thoroughfare outside New England." To the frontier its large homes and quaint row houses brought an air of east coast urbanity. Roads throughout this route get very little traffic—even on weekends in summer. The urban riding is interesting, and the rural riding delightful.

The ride starts on Geneva's South Main Street, at the campus of Hobart and William Smith Colleges.

0.0 From the Hobart College campus, ride north (with the lake to your right) on South Main Street, Route 14.

Geneva College was founded in 1822. Its name was changed in 1851 to honor its founder, Bishop John Henry Hobart. The oldest buildings, Geneva Hall and Trinity Hall, face both the college quadrangle and South Main Street. Hobart's associated women's college, William Smith, was

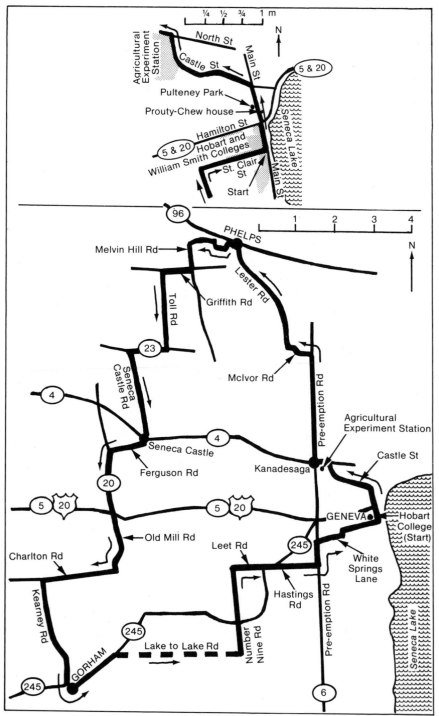

founded in 1906.

A few of the impressive old houses along Main Street are college residences, but many more are still in private hands. Through the nineteenth century South Main Street maintained a decidedly genteel atmosphere, begun by transplanted southern gentry and continued by a disproportionate number of retired ministers and well-born spinsters. The Prouty-Chew House (1825) at 543 South Main Street can be visited Tuesday through Saturday 1:30 to 4:30 p.m. Its furnishings reflect Federal through Victorian styles, and the lower floor is home to the Geneva Historical Society.

A hundred or so yards downhill from the Prouty-Chew House is Pulteney Park (where cattle grazed until 1862), laid out by Captain Charles Williamson, agent for Sir William Pulteney and his English associates, who then owned much of western New York. Behind the park, the Pulteney Apartments contain some of the fabric of Williamson's 1796 Geneva Hotel, long a marvel of elegance. Williamson had hanging gardens planted on the precipice facing the lake and decreed that the east side of Main Street should not be built upon, so that hotel guests could have an unobstructed view of the lake. The row houses that did come after his time mitigate the loss of the lake view with their own charm.

On the right side of South Main Street a historical marker notes the place where Elizabeth Blackwell became the first woman to graduate from a medical school in America. The Geneva Medical College she attended was part of Hobart which, of course, admitted only men. Faculty and students assumed Blackwell's application to be a joke, and it was accepted in that spirit. On arrival, she was advised to leave immediately; she refused, and in two years she had her medical degree. Dr. Blackwell soon founded the New York City Infirmary for Women and Children, and in time she received many honors, both in America and in her native England.

0.9 Turn LEFT at the third set of traffic lights, onto Castle Street. Two left turns are possible at this corner; make the less sharp left, so that the library is to your right.

There are several restaurants and luncheonettes in Geneva, including, at this intersection, Wing Tai, one of the few Chinese restaurants in the Finger Lakes. You'll pass a small supermarket on Castle Street and will find other food stores and a restaurant or two in the villages along this route.

Just under a mile along Castle Street a marker identifies the Smith Observatory of Dr. William Brooks, a self-taught nineteenth century astronomer who discovered twenty-seven comets, more than anyone else.

2.2   At the traffic light, turn LEFT onto North Street.

To the right at this corner is a fine example of an octagon house, an original American style popular in the 1850s. The design's creator, phrenologist Orson Fowler, promised economy of materials, functional interiors, good views, and improved health of occupants.

The campus-like area to the left is part of the New York State Agricultural Experiment Station, a branch of the State University of New York and Cornell University. In 1882 the station began research to benefit New York's leading industry, agriculture. Emphasis is on fruit and vegetable experiments, with departments ranging from cytology to food technology. Six Geneva-developed apples are among the top twenty in the state; of these the best known are Empire, Cortland, and Macoun. There is a small public display area in the lobby of the Entomology and Plant Pathology Building.

2.5   Turn RIGHT at the traffic light onto County Road 6, Pre-emption Road.

Past the Mobil station, a sign on the left marks the site of Kanadesaga, where Sir William Johnson built a fort for England's Indian allies in 1756. The village was once the home of the Seneca's chief sachem. Behind the gas station an Indian burial mound can be discerned.

The Pre-emption line you are riding along, on County Road 6, dates from a 1786 compromise between Massachusetts and New York, both claiming sovereignty to what is now western New York. The deal worked out gave New York sovereignty to the region, but allowed Massachusetts pre-emptive rights to sell the land west of the line. Massachusetts quickly did sell, though the buyers were cheated somewhat by a surveying error (said to be deliberate). County Road 6 actually runs along what's called Old Pre-emption Line; the true line runs a couple of miles to the east. The narrow wedge between the lines was referred to as "the Gore".

5.1 Turn LEFT onto McIvor Road.

5.7 Make the first RIGHT turn possible, onto Lester Road (unsignposted).

Soon, what seems like miles of perfect white fencing outlines fields and paddocks to your left. Here are raised Tennessee Walking Horses, a large breed based on the Morgan. Known as "easy-gaited," a properly trained Walking Horse doesn't trot but moves swiftly in a smooth "running walk." The breed was developed in the South for use on the soft footing of cotton plantations.

Two miles farther, a sign marks the location of the Red House Observatory where Dr. William Brooks discovered eleven comets between 1881 and 1888, the year he moved to Geneva.

8.7 Turn LEFT at the T-junction onto Route 96 West.

The village of Phelps—which for some unknown reason was first called Woodpecker City—is named in honor of Oliver Phelps, who, with Nathaniel Gorham, purchased in 1788 from the state of Massachusetts almost all of what is now New York west of Seneca Lake. A sweetener in the deal, allowing Phelps and Gorham to pay in depreciated Massachusetts securities, turned sour when Alexander Hamilton led the federal government to assume the debts of the states. The value of Massachusetts notes skyrocketed. By 1790 Phelps and Gorham had failed to make payments, and Massachusetts took back about two-thirds of the original purchase. Most of the remaining third (1.25 million acres) was sold by the partners to Robert Morris, the financier of the American Revolution and a friend of George Washington. In 1791 Morris sold at a profit to the English syndicate headed by Sir William Pulteney.

The Pulteney interests, led by their daring, dashing, and extravagant land agent, Scottish Captain Charles Williamson, left the greatest mark on western New York's early development. But Oliver Phelps and Nathaniel Gorham opened in Canandaigua the first land office in America, and both gave their names to Ontario County villages.

9.3 In the village of Phelps, turn LEFT at the traffic light onto Church Street.

A block along the left, the library has made wonderful use of an 1849 stone church designed by David Bates Douglass, an American polymath who also planned Brooklyn's Greenwood Cemetery and the New York City water supply system, surveyed part of the United States-Canadian border, taught mathematics at West Point and Hobart, and was president of Kenyon College.

The high point of the year in this cabbage town, home of

Geneva's Agricultural Experiment Station concentrates research on fruits and vegetables; it has produced several successful apple varieties.

the Silver Floss Kraut Company, is the Sauerkraut Festival, held every year in early August. Special features of the two-day event include the speed sauerkraut-eating contest and the cutting of the sauerkraut cake—with free pieces to the first 1,000 takers.

9.5 Turn RIGHT at the Stop sign onto Park Street.
Along this street is a shady village park.

9.7 At the T-junction, turn RIGHT onto William Street.

9.9 Turn LEFT and cross the railroad tracks. You should now be on Ontario Street.

10.4 Turn LEFT at the Stop sign onto Melvin Hill Road.

11.1 Turn RIGHT onto Griffith Road.

11.8 Turn LEFT onto Toll Road.
It seems surprising that a toll could have been charged on such a rural road, but in the early years of the nineteenth century the state lacked resources to serve its burgeoning western frontier, and private companies were licensed to build roads and turn a profit where they could.

13.8 At the T-junction, turn RIGHT onto County Road 23.

14.8 At the top of the hill, turn LEFT onto Wheat Road, also called Seneca Castle Road.
The hill you just climbed brought you up the steep west side of a drumlin; riding south you enjoy a long, gentle downhill.

In the hamlet of Seneca Castle no turns are made. "Castle" does not signify a fortification; it was simply a term the Dutch and English colonists applied to Indian villages, regardless of their military usefulness.

In late summer and autumn you may see, and on warm days, smell, cabbages in fields, or on roadside stands. Some bounce from over-laden trucks; but carrying a huge commercial head home on a bike requires ingenuity. A few years ago a Seneca Castle man developed a mechanical cabbage picker, which is now manufactured there. Until recently it was common to see work crews loading ten-pound cabbages into trucks with long pitchforks, surely one of the toughest of harvest chores.

17.0 Just as houses yield to farmland, turn RIGHT onto Ferguson Road.

17.9 Turn LEFT at the T-junction, onto County Road 20.

19.5 Continue STRAIGHT across Routes 5 and 20 onto Old Mill Road.

Along Flint Creek we have seen wild turkeys. They are slimmer than the domesticated variety and move quickly through the underbrush. The best chance to see the birds is in early spring, before leaves are fully out.

20.9 Turn RIGHT onto Charlton Road.

21.6 Continue STRAIGHT across Goose Street on Depew Road (the new name for Charlton Road).

22.8 Turn LEFT at Kearney Road.

24.6 Cross Lake to Lake Road, and continue STRAIGHT.

25.5 Turn LEFT at the Stop sign onto Route 245 (unsignposted).

25.7 At the corner in the middle of Gorham, turn LEFT to follow Route 245 North. At the fork, keep RIGHT, to stay on Route 245.

27.0 Turn RIGHT onto Lake to Lake Road.

The route described below is unpaved for about one mile. If you want to avoid this section, continue on Route 245 for about four more miles, then turn left onto Number Nine Road to rejoin the route at the 31.0 mile point.

28.1 Continue STRAIGHT across Little Church Road; from here the road is unpaved for one mi e.

30.2 At the second Stop sign, continue STRAIGHT onto the paved Route 14A. In about 150 yards turn LEFT onto Number Nine Road.

The unusual name of this road dates from the survey of the Phelps-Gorham Purchase of 1788, when townships had only numbers.

31.0 At the Stop sign, continue STRAIGHT across Route 245.

32.4 Turn RIGHT onto Leet Road.

33.3 Continue STRAIGHT at the Yield sign.

33.6 Keep RIGHT at the fork, taking Hastings Road, as Routes 245 and 14A go left.

If you are traveling between August and October you will shortly see acres of dahlias to the right. Legg Dahlia Gardens is one of the fifty or so nurseries for which Geneva was once famous. Visitors are welcome daily from 8:00 a.m. to sunset; admission is free.

34.7 Turn LEFT at the Stop sign onto County Road 6, Pre-emption Road.

35.2 Between the brick pillars, turn RIGHT onto White Springs Lane.

From 1790 White Springs Farm's 1,600 acres was the anomalous home of "Virginia plantation life, modified by climate and the laws of the state affecting the holding of slaves." Later it was owned by a succession of wealthy gentlemen farmers, and had prize-winning breeding stock of shorthorns and Guernseys. The present buildings date from 1900-1902.

35.9 At the T-junction, turn LEFT.

36.1 Turn RIGHT onto St. Clair Street.

37.0 Soon you'll see the athletic fields of Hobart-William Smith. You will reach your starting point in another mile or so.

For an elegant end to the day, you might visit Belhurst Castle, about two miles south of Hobart on Route 14. Formerly a casino, this outstanding 1890 Richardsonian Romanesque mansion has six guest rooms "for the discriminating traveler." Lunch and dinner are served daily in season, and the spacious lawns and lake view are open to all (315-781-0201). More modest accommodations can be found at Virginia Deane's Bed and Breakfast, opposite the Hobart campus at 168 Hamilton Street (315-789-6152).

Nearby bed-and-breakfasts include:

LaFayette B&B, 107 LaFayette Avenue, Geneva, NY (315-781-0068)

Bicycle Shops

Canandaigua Bicycle Center, 143 South Main Street, Canandaigua, NY (716-394-6150)

Geneva Bicycle Center, 493 Exchange Street, Geneva, NY (315-789-5922)

Park Avenue Bike Shop, 28 Lake Shore Drive, Canandaigua, NY (716-394-1530)

5

Canandaigua—Vine Valley

27 miles; moderate cycling
Level to rolling terrain with long, gradual hills
County maps: Ontario, Yates

Fine views of lake and vineyards abound in this tour along the east side of sixteen-mile-long Canandaigua Lake. The first half of the ride parallels the lake shore, with a convenient lunch or rest stop at the appropriately named Vine Valley. (An optional diversion offers a few more miles of lakeside riding south of the valley.) From Vine Valley the route climbs inland to the village of Rushville, birthplace of the Oregon Trail pioneer Marcus Whitman. A high and little-used ridge road leads back to the city of Canandaigua, affording excellent views of the northern part of the lake and an exhilarating freewheel down a long, gentle hill. There are opportunities for swimming and fishing along the lake's east side and at its north end, where the tour starts and finishes. Those with time to spare can hike nature trails on the campus of the Community College of the Finger Lakes. Outdoor concerts by the Rochester Philharmonic Orchestra are given on summer weekends on the campus overlooking the lake.

The tour begins at Roseland Bowl, located at the southeast corner of the city of Canandaigua on Lake Shore Drive, the road bordering the lake's north end.

0.0   From Roseland Bowl ride east on Lake Shore Drive with the lake on your right.

The land between road and lake was the site of Roseland Park, opened in 1926. Built beyond reach of rail and trolley lines, it was one of the first amusement parks in the country dependent on roads and automobiles. A carousel with a versatile calliope provided a turn-of-the-century atmosphere.

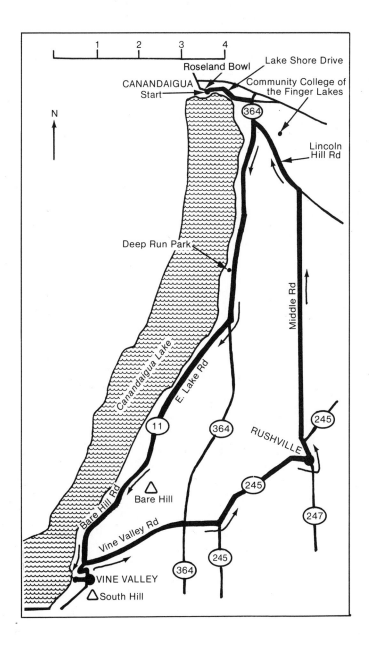

There are several eateries along Lake Shore Drive. Those wishing to carry food with them will find several supermarkets in town. The most extravagant selection of deli, bakery, gourmet, and natural foods is at Wegmans (open 24 hours) at the corner of Lake Shore Drive and Main Street, about a half-mile west of Roseland.

0.4   At the traffic light turn RIGHT onto East Lake Road, Route 364 South.

Route 364 can get an uncomfortable amount of traffic on summer weekends, and its shoulder is intermittent; the good news is that you'll be on this road for less than five miles. Three miles along Route 364 is Deep Run Park, where facilities include picnic tables, rest rooms, and drinking fountains. The major attraction of Deep Run is its bathing beach; fishing may be possible in spring and fall, or when no swimmers are present.

One-half mile farther on you'll see Thendara, a restaurant overlooking the lake. Shortly after 1900 it was built as a retirement home by John Raines, a State Senator and U.S. Congressman; the fourteen-room mansion was completed just before his death. Thendara's special feature is its Boathouse, where light meals and drinks are served from noon to 10:00 p.m. seven days a week from May to October.

5.1   At the fork, go RIGHT onto County Road 11, East Lake Road.

About two and a half miles down County Road 11, a mile-long hill begins that takes you up about 350 feet. Here the road climbs a flank of Bare Hill (el. 1,540′) which, with neighboring South Hill (el. 1,893′), figures prominently in the mythology of the Seneca Indians.

Bare Hill, called Genundawah by the Senecas, was sacred to the tribe. According to legend, the hill was once encircled by an enormous two-headed serpent that devoured the Seneca inhabitants. A young warrior, instructed in a dream to string his bow with the hair of his young sister, finally slew the serpent. In its death throes the serpent tumbled down the hillside, tearing up the vegetation and disgorging the heads of the Senecas it had eaten. Although wooded now, Bare Hill is said to have been free of trees when white men first saw it. The Seneca rite of lighting ceremonial fires yearly on Bare Hill is echoed by lake property owners who, signaled by a flare atop Bare Hill, light a Ring of Fire around Canandaigua Lake on the Saturday evening before Labor Day.

Soon after Bare Hill turns from antagonist to helper it becomes clear that the name Vine Valley is not fanciful. Vineyards carpet the gentle bowl of the valley floor. Depending on the season, you may see workers tying up vines before the growing season, large green leaves hiding tiny grape clusters, or heavy masses of golden, russet or purple grapes. On warm autumn days the smell, as well as the sight, is heavenly.

11.6 Turn RIGHT at the T-junction onto Vine Valley Road (unsign-posted). Caution: Vine Valley Road drops sharply and, in about 100 feet, makes a 180-degree turn.

A state historical marker at this junction notes the 1922 excavation of an Indian burial ground in Vine Valley. It is believed to be a grave site of early Woodland Indians of the Adena culture, thought to have migrated from Ohio, bringing with them an appreciation of finely made stone objects and a tradition of building mound graves. The arti-facts of pottery, bone, antler, and stone recovered from the Vine Valley graves are dated between 500 B.C. and A.D. 500.

11.8 At the Vine Valley United Methodist Church (1891) turn RIGHT and ride down to the lake shore.

The former Robeson General Store, near the lake, was already a Vine Valley landmark by the turn of the century. It once housed dances, church socials, and long winter chats. The property was purchased by the town, which has installed picnic tables and a swimming beach beside the old building.

In the old days, Vine Valley was an important stop for Canandaigua Lake steamboats bringing goods to the store and picnickers to Willow Grove, a recreation area that is now a trailer park. Holiday-makers could buy a special ticket at the Canandaigua City Pier good for a day's outing at Willow Grove, and return to Canandaigua on a moonlight cruise. In addition to summer revelers, the steamers once carried grapes, apples, and other produce to Canandaigua and thence to other cities. Travel by water became so much easier than by land that the steamers put the Canandaigua-to-Naples stagecoach out of business. In our century improved roads and automobiles made land travel more efficient, and most of the steamers disappeared by the First World War.

12.1 From the lake shore, retrace your route to the church corner and turn LEFT. Follow the road around the 180-degree turn, up the steep grade, keeping to the right. Do *not* turn left onto the road which brought you to Vine Valley. As you climb, Bare Hill is to your left, South Hill to your right.

For a few more miles of quiet lakeside riding, one can add the following diversion: Turn right, instead of left, at the Vine Valley church. Follow this road as it bends right, down to the lake, and then left. This road dead ends, so traffic is light. Just over two miles from Vine Valley is Whiskey Point, where a still once operated. A whiskey scow once sunk near the Point, and is presumably still there. One can ride for about three miles before it is necessary to turn around and return to Vine Valley. Although there is no official public access, cyclists interested in fishing can ask permission of lake shore residents.

14.9 Continue STRAIGHT, crossing Route 364.

A well-preserved one-room brick school dated 1874 is located on the northwest corner of this intersection, known locally as Overacker Corners. It was in use until 1937.

15.7 At the bottom of the hill, turn LEFT at the Stop sign onto Route 245 North.

Along this stretch you'll pass the Marcus Whitman public school, named in honor of Rushville's most famous son.

18.2 Turn LEFT at the T-junction onto Rushville's Main Street, which is also Routes 245 and 247.

Rushville's Federal Hollow Market is located a hundred feet to the right at this corner. The village was originally called Federal Hollow; the name was changed during the War of 1812 when the Federalist Party opposed the locally popular war. The new name honored Dr. Benjamin Rush, a signer of the Declaration of Independence and a Democrat.

On the left, one block after turning onto Main Street, you'll see a marker commemorating the birthplace of Dr. Marcus Whitman, born on September 4, 1802. Whitman traveled the Oregon Trail twice, the second time with his wife, Narcissa Prentiss, one of the first two white women to cross the Rockies. More of Whitman's story is recounted in Tour 19.

18.6 At the end of Main Street, take the LEFT fork, following a straight course as Route 245-247 bears right. The uphill lasts about three-quarters of a mile.

19.3 At the crest of the hill, take the RIGHT fork, Middle Road.

24.1 Turn LEFT at the askew T-junction, onto Lincoln Hill Road.

Soon you will have good views to the foot of Canandaigua Lake, including Squaw Island, one of two islands in the Finger Lakes and the smallest state park in New York. Legend has it that Seneca women and children were hidden on the island from General Sullivan's Expedition of 1779.

26.0 Turn RIGHT at the Stop sign onto Route 364 North.

About two hundred yards before this corner, a turn to the right leads to the campus of the Community College of the Finger Lakes, summer home of the Rochester Philharmonic Orchestra. The concert shell sits at the foot of a hill which overlooks the lake. Thousands come on weekend evenings in July and August to listen to the concert and to picnic, sample local wine, and watch the sun set over the lake. Lawn tickets are $12-16 for adults. Program information can be obtained by calling the orchestra at 716-222-5000 or the college at 716-394-7198.

The college also has two marked nature trails, tennis

Robeson's waterside general store was a Vine Valley landmark from the late nineteenth century until the 1980s.

courts, and an air-conditioned cafeteria and library. Cafeteria summer hours are 8:00 a.m. to 1:00 p.m. and 6:00 p.m. to 8:00 p.m. weekdays.

At this corner is the Lincoln Hill Inn, serving continental specialties to concert-goers and other guests.

26.4 Turn LEFT at the traffic light onto Lake Shore Drive.

26.8 You should now be back at Roseland Bowl.

Nearby you can swim at Kershaw Park located just west of Roseland on Lake Shore Drive. Farther along in this direction are several snack bars and restaurants, including the Federal-style Colonial Inn. In operation since 1845, the inn used to be called the Lake Breeze House, and catered to rail and steam-boat passengers making transfers at the nearby City Pier. The Pier itself dates from 1845 when $1,000 was spent on its construction. Makeshift boat houses lined the west side of the Pier until a 1903 beautification scheme had them removed to the lateral arms where they remain—picturesque, charming, or dilapidated, depending on your viewpoint.

Short launch tours of the lake operate from the Sheraton Inn (adjacent to the City Pier). For schedules and fares call Captain Gray's Boat Tours, 716-394-5270. Boat rentals or fishing charters can be arranged at the base of the pier at Seager Marine, 716-394-1372. Farther out on the pier you'll find sailboard rentals. Those seeking more immobile pursuits can feed the ducks, or browse at the Waterfront Art Festival, held at the City Pier annually on the first weekend in August.

Nearby bed-and-breakfasts include:

Clawson's B&B, 3615 Lincoln Hill Road, Canandaigua, NY (716-396-1947)

Habersham Country Inn, 6124 Route 5 and 20, Canandaigua, NY (716-394-1510)

Lakeview Farm B&B, 4761 Route 364, Rushville, NY (716-554-6973)

Oliver Phelps Country Inn, 252 North Main Street, Canandaigua, NY (716-396-1650)

Wilder Tavern Country Inn, 5648 North Bloomfield Road, Canandaigua, NY (716-394-8132)

Bicycle shops

Canandaigua Bicycle Center, 143 South Main Street, Canandaigua, NY (716-394-6150)

Park Avenue Bike Shop, 28 Lake Shore Drive, Canandaigua, NY (716-394-1530)

6

Canandaigua—City and Lake

18 miles; easy to moderate cycling
Flat terrain with some low hills
County map: Ontario

In 1832 Englishwoman Frances Trollope wrote of Canandaigua: "It is as pretty a village as ever man contrived to build. Every house is surrounded by an ample garden ... and half buried in roses." Earlier, in 1804, Robert Munro reported that some of Canandaigua's houses were "elegant," and that "many of its inhabitants are wealthy in circumstances." Along the city's wide and shaded streets, many fine houses in a great variety of architectural styles are still seen, including the much-visited Sonnenberg Gardens and Mansion. But city quickly gives way to farm and orchard. This route also visits the quiet village of Cheshire and includes several miles of cool riding along the shore of Canandaigua Lake, passing a public swimming beach. For combining historic and architectural interest with country scenery and pleasant riding, it is a tour hard to equal.

The ride begins in the City of Canandaigua in front of the County Court House on North Main Street. The golden-domed court house is visible for miles around.

0.0 From the front of the court house ride north (uphill) on North Main Street.

The present Ontario County Court House dates from 1857-58. Its most famous trial occured in 1873 when Susan B. Anthony was found guilty of voting and was fined $100. Anthony actually voted in Rochester, where her house is now maintained as a museum, but a change of venue brought the case to Canandaigua. In a move of doubtful legality, the judge dismissed the jury and directed a guilty verdict, but the fine was never paid, nor was any other punishment exacted.

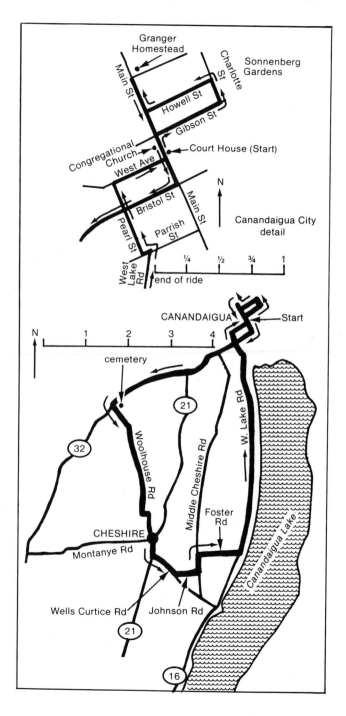

Granger Homestead

Sonnenberg Gardens

Charlotte St

Main St

Howell St

Gibson St

Congregational Church

Court House (Start)

West Ave

N

Bristol St

Main St

Canandaigua City detail

Pearl St

Parrish St

West Lake Rd

end of ride

¼   ½   ¾   1

CANANDAIGUA

Start

N

1   2   3   4

cemetery

21

Woolhouse Rd

32

Middle Cheshire Rd

W. Lake Rd

Foster Rd

Canandaigua Lake

CHESHIRE

Montanye Rd

Wells Curtice Rd

Johnson Rd

21

16

Just up the street at 55 North Main is a 1913 Georgian Revival building housing the Ontario County Historical Society. In addition to its changing exhibits, the society provides several brochures with detailed architectural tours of the city, plus other publications on local history. The building is open afternoons Tuesday through Saturday from 10:00 a.m. to 5:00 p.m. Admission is free.

0.2 Turn RIGHT at the traffic light onto Gibson Street.

Number 29, the first of three impressive Federal-style houses on Gibson Street, was once the home of Myron Holley Clark (1806–1892), the only Temperance governor of New York and the father of Mary Clark Thompson, benefactress of the city and creator of Sonnenberg Gardens.

0.8 Turn LEFT onto Charlotte Street. This corner also has a sign to the VA Medical Center and Sonnenberg Gardens.

Charlotte Street is shaded by plane trees planted by one of Sonnenberg's landscape architects, John Handrahan, in 1903.

Mary Clark married Frederick Ferris Thompson, a founder of the First National Bank of New York, in 1857. By 1887 they had completed Sonnenberg as their summer home; the elaborate gardens were added by the widowed Mrs. Thompson from 1902 to 1916. The mansion shows various architectural influences—unified by a style perhaps best called Pre-Income Tax Opulent. Refurbished and refurnished, the house is a fascinating Victorian testament to how the other one percent lived. On Sonnenberg's fifty acres the Italian, Rose, Japanese, Colonial, and Rock Gardens have been restored to their former glory. The Italian Garden is filled with tulips in May, and continues with begonias and other annuals through the summer; the roses peak in late June. Sonnenberg Gardens and Mansion are open daily 9:30 a.m. to 5:30 p.m. May through mid-October, with special musical and theatrical performances scheduled occasionally. Admission is $4.25 for adults and $1.25 for those under eighteen. Sonnenberg's Peach House Restaurant, in a former greenhouse, and Garden Cafe, with outdoor tables, serve light lunches and elaborate desserts from 11:30 a.m. to 3:30 p.m. May through September. Nearby, the Canandaigua Wine Company operates a complimentary wine tasting room in what was once the estate's cannery.

1.0 Turn LEFT onto Howell Street. On your right at this corner are the massive wrought iron gates of the entrance to Sonnenberg.

Howell Street is one of the most pleasant residential streets in the city. Altogether its houses provide a convenient compendium of popular nineteenth century styles: Federal, Greek Revival, Italianate, Second Empire, Eastlake, Tudor, Queen Anne.

1.6 Turn RIGHT at the T-junction onto North Main Street.

1.9 The Granger Homestead, to your right, is as far up Main Street as this tour extends. When you have seen or visited the Homestead, make a U-TURN and ride south, downhill, back toward the business district.

The Granger Homestead at 295 North Main Street was built about 1816 for Gideon Granger, Postmaster General under Presidents Jefferson and Monroe. This predominantly Federal-style building was also home to Gideon's son, Francis, another Postmaster General, and later it housed a girls' school. The elegant interior is described on guided tours given Tuesday through Saturday from 10:00 a.m. to 5:00 p.m. and 1:00 to 5:00 p.m. on Sunday. Admission is $2.50 for adults and $1.00 for children under sixteen. (A combined Granger-Sonnenberg ticket costs $6.00 for adults.) The Homestead's carriage house displays the second-largest collection of horse-drawn vehicles in New York. It includes the carriage of Jemima Wilkinson, one of the odd religious figures of the region, who settled in 1791 with her followers near Keuka Lake. This self-styled prophetess called herself the Publick Universal Friend, and the initials UF can still be barely discerned on the rear and door of her carriage.

A short distance down Main Street from the Granger Homestead is the Elm Manor Nursing Home at number 210. The front protion of the complex was built in 1797 for Peter B. Porter, but it was home to several men of note—a United States Senator, and two Presidential Cabinet secretaries. Peter Porter was Secretary of War under John Q. Adams; he was also an influential early backer of the Erie Canal and later contributed greatly to the development of the Buffalo area. Senator Elbridge G. Lapham is best remembered for leading Senate ratification of the Geneva Con-

Canandaigua's City Pier is a convenient place from which to watch activity on the lake.

vention in 1882. John Spencer had a successful legal and political career (holding two cabinet posts), but he is chiefly remembered for being the unfortunate father of a more unfortunate son, Philip Spencer. Philip was born here, walked across the street to school, and spent several desultory years at Hobart College in Geneva. While his father was Secretary of War, Philip joined the Navy, was involved in strange goings-on aboard ship, and was precipitously hanged at sea on December 1, 1842 on the charge of attempted mutiny. The incident produced a sensation in its time, and provided Herman Melville with the story-line for his novelette, *Billy Budd*.

The Congregational Church at 58 North Main Street is perhaps the most interesting public building in the city. Built in 1812, its harmonious rectangular form is enlivened by an arched entranceway. The fine interior features box pews with the original doors and hinges. Though it has been known as the "Old Brick," it seems that the church has always been painted, often necessary to protect weak, locally pressed brick from weathering. The father of social critic Max Eastman was pastor here in the late nineteenth century, and Max was born at the parsonage (built *c.* 1830) at 116 East Gibson Street, behind the small park-like square.

On the right, at the corner of West Avenue, is the City and Town Hall building. It was built in 1824 and served as the Court House until the present one was constructed.

2.8   When you have passed through most of the business district, you'll come to a traffic light at Bristol Street where you make a RIGHT turn. Continue STRAIGHT on Bristol out of town.

Near the edge of town, just before Bristol Street goes briefly downhill, you may notice a bronze plaque on a stone gatepost to the left. It notes that the Sullivan-Clinton campaign to destroy the Iroquois allied with the British, passed here on September 11 and 18, 1779. The gateposts lead to Brigham Hall, built in 1855 as a private hospital for the insane. Later used as a nursing home and now converted into apartments, much of the hospital's careful landscaping can still be seen. From Canandaigua, Sullivan's army marched over the hills to Honeoye, and two days later it reached the Genesee River. For the next three or so miles our route roughly follows the army's line of march.

4.5 Go STRAIGHT on County Road 32 as Route 21 turns to the left.

6.5 Turn LEFT onto Woolhouse Road.

At this corner is a cemetery with graves dating from the beginning of white settlement in the area.

If you want to extend the tour by about four miles to include some challenging hill climbing, do not turn left on Woolhouse Road. Instead, continue straight on County Road 32 another four miles, turning left there onto Montanye Road. Following this road will take you over high hills and into the village of Cheshire.

9.6 Turn RIGHT at the T-junction onto Route 21 South.

To the right is a former public school that now houses The Company Store which has an excellent selection of food, including freshly prepared sandwiches. It's open in summer daily from 7:00 a.m. to 10:00 p.m. There are picnic tables by the playing field behind the school, or you can eat at tables in one of the old school rooms.

10.0 Continue through the village of Cheshire and turn LEFT just before the last house on the left onto Wells-Curtice Road (not signposted).

10.7 Turn LEFT onto Johnson Road.

Along Johnson Road killdeer are often seen and heard. When they run before taking flight, their white wing patches show clearly. Their piping whistle is often the loudest sound heard here.

11.3 Turn LEFT at the T-junction onto Middle Cheshire Road.

11.7 Turn RIGHT onto Foster Road, also following the sign to Notre Dame (retreat house).

The lower half of Foster Road passes between abandoned orchards—apple, pear, peach, cherry. In blossom time, about mid-May, it combines the pleasures of an Impressionist painting and a perfume distillery.

Care is needed as Foster Road comes to an end; the final hundred or so feet are very steep, and the intersection is usually slippery with loose sand and gravel.

12.6 Turn LEFT at the T-junction onto West Lake Road.

Along West Lake Road you might note a couple of cobblestone houses. This is south of the area where cobblestone building was common in the second third of the nineteenth century, and it is likely that the cobbles were carted here from a spot near the Lake Ontario shore.

Two-and-a-half miles farther, where Butler Road enters from the left, is a small public swimming area. The one-room school across the road had classes until the 1960s and is now used for a youth summer recreation program.

A half-mile north of Butler Road is the Canandaigua Yacht Club. Races are scheduled for most Sunday mornings. If you're interested in watching these often colorful events, or in perhaps offering to crew, schedule details can be had by calling 716-394-9800 in Canandaigua, or 716-924-3100 in Rochester.

16.9 Turn LEFT at the traffic light onto Parrish Street, and in 75 feet, at another traffic light, turn RIGHT onto South Pearl Street.

17.6 Turn RIGHT at the second traffic light onto West Avenue.

On the right, opposite Apples market, you'll pass Canandaigua's Pioneer Cemetery. Among the oldest graves is that of Oliver Phelps of the famous Phelps-Gorham Purchase which opened western New York to settlement.

18.0 Continuing along West Avenue to the traffic light will bring you to Main Street and the Ontario County Court House.

Nearby bed-and-breakfasts include:

Clawson's B&B, 3615 Lincoln Hill Road, Canandaigua, NY (716-396-1947)

Habersham Country Inn, 6124 Route 5 and 20, Canandaigua, NY (716-394-1510)

J.P. Morgan House, 2920 Smith Road, Canandaigua, NY (716-394-9232)

Oliver Phelps Country Inn, 252 North Main Street, Canandaigua, NY (716-396-1650)

Wilder Tavern B&B, 5648 North Bloomfield Road, Canandaigua, NY (716-394-8132)

Bicycle shops

Canandaigua Bicycle Center, 143 South Main Street, Canandaigua, NY (716-394-6150)

Park Avenue Bike Shop, 28 Lake Shore Drive, Canandaigua, NY (716-394-1530)

7

The Bristol Hills

24 miles; moderate to strenuous cycling
Rolling to hilly terrain with some level sections
County map: Ontario

The Bristol Hills form the highest and some of the most rugged, attractive scenery in the Finger Lakes. Their once-sparse farm population has broadened recently to include independent craftspeople and antique dealers who have found niches in the steep-sided valleys and wooded hilltops. This tour links quiet villages via roads that give the cyclist strenuous climbs rewarded by distant views and swift descents. It passes a downhill ski center said to have the highest vertical drop between the Adirondacks and the Rockies. Leaving a road high above Canandaigua Lake, you drop rapidly, to enjoy a couple miles of shore riding along the lake's most affluent "cottage" area. Quiet back roads are used, except for a few miles in the Bristol Valley and a short distance on Route 21.

The tour starts in the village of Cheshire at the converted school on the west side of Route 21.

0.0 From the front of the old school building, ride south on Route 21 for two hundred yards until you come to Goodale Road. Turn RIGHT at this junction.

Closed as a school in 1965, this building is now occupied by The Company Store, which provides the makings of a fine picnic, including cold drinks, hot coffee, and freshly made sandwiches. Company Store summer hours are 6:30 a.m. to 10:00 p.m. every day of the week. You'll find picnic tables behind the school near the playing field, and more tables in the town park on Goodale Road. If you prefer, you can eat indoors in a former school room, or shop for antiques upstairs.

Cheshire straddles a state highway, but the pace of the village is more aptly characterized by the dogs that saunter unhurriedly along its main street. First called Klipknocket, it seems appropriate that the village was afterwards known as Idle Corners, the final name change

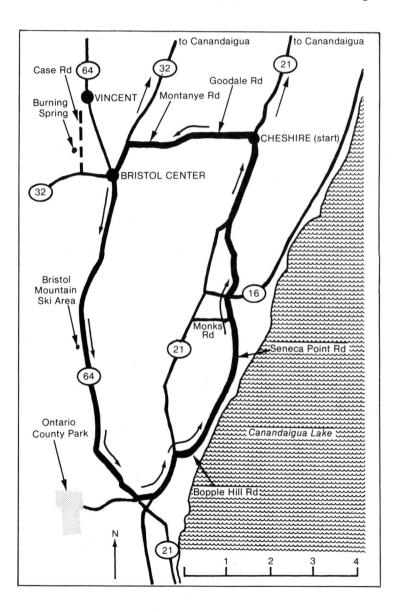

coming at the behest of immigrants from Cheshire in Connecticut.

Cheshire has two other antique shops. Inside one called The Emporium it is dark and cool, with wainscoting and the smell of old wood. The building once served as a grange hall, and was a theater and community center in a time when villages such as Cheshire were more isolated and self-sufficient. You can see the old stage at the rear of The Emporium, and high on its walls are advertising placards for performances in the early years of this century.

Goodale Road climbs about 400 feet in the first mile after leaving Cheshire, reaching an elevation of 1,420 feet. After the crest is passed, Goodale Road is called Montanye Road; this is because each road dead ended until recently, when the two were linked by the road over the hills.

3.1 At the T-junction, turn LEFT onto County Road 32 (unsign-posted).

In a few yards you'll be looking into the Bristol Valley and facing a nearly mile-long downhill. Don't let generally good paving lull you into freewheeling too fast.

To visit another antique shop you can turn right, instead of left, at the T-junction and ride for a half-mile to the Little Grey Schoolhouse, run by a woman who once attended the old one-room school that is now her shop.

3.9 At the Stop sign at the bottom of the hill, turn LEFT onto Route 64 South.

Food supplies can be obtained here at the Bristol Hills Country Store, which is across from The Wood Box, an antique and art gallery.

The French explorer La Salle is said to have visited Bristol Valley in 1669 while searching for the Mississippi's source. It is said that local Indians took La Salle, perhaps the first white man they had seen, to their miraculous Burning Spring. To visit the site of the Burning Spring, go straight across Route 64 at the bottom of the long hill, continuing west on County Road 32. In seven-tenths of a mile turn right onto the unpaved Case Road. A half-mile farther you'll see a marker for the Burning Spring just beyond a small stream. When Captain Basil Hall, a British traveler, did what you are doing in 1827 he noted that "on reaching the spot, we discovered a spring to be sure, but could see no flames .... I was beginning to feel that awkward sort of distrust which accompanies the suspicion of being quizzed, and sent on a fool's errand; when behold! the air caught fire, and in a few minutes, we had a row of natural gas lights blazing in a style worthy of Pall-Mall ..." It is believed that natural gas escapes beneath water and bubbles to the surface, where it can be ignited. We've never seen it done, but if you want to try you should ask permission at the house, as the stream is on private property.

From the Burning Spring, retrace your route to the intersection with Route 64, and there turn south. In all, this diversion adds 2.8 miles.

The Bristol Valley is a typical glacial valley, with a flat bottom and steep, wooded sides. A surprising amount of what appears to be useful, easily worked bottom land is unfarmed scrub and brush. Some blame this on over-grazing by sheep in the nineteenth century. Two miles north of the village of Bristol Center was another called Muttonville; between 1830 and 1850 it had the nation's largest sheep slaughterhouse, and the Bristol Valley was temporary home to some 50,000 sheep. Today Mutton-ville has been renamed Vincent after a pioneer physician, and almost no sheep are seen.

Halfway down the valley you pass the Bristol Mountain

Top racers from the U.S. and Canada enter the Canandaigua Cup Bicycle Race, held on the Sunday after Labor Day.

Ski Center, offering downhill skiers the highest vertical drop between the Adirondacks and the Rockies.

14.2 In the hamlet of Bristol Springs, turn LEFT at Gannett Hill Road.

Provisions can be obtained here at Taylor's General Store.

If you turn right instead of left at this corner you can visit Ontario County Park atop 2,256-foot-high Gannett Hill, the highest elevation in the Finger Lakes and the site of the University of Rochester's Mees Observatory. It's a hard climb of about a mile and a half to reach the park, but if you're interested in camping, the setting and facilities are ideal. The park also has picnic tables and shelters, rest rooms and hiking trails. Orange tree blazes mark the Bristol Hill spur of the Finger Lakes Trail, which snakes east-west for a hundred miles or so across the southern Finger Lakes. The most striking views are in the vicinity of the Jump-off, to which there are many signs. From there you look down into West Hollow, a glacial valley narrower and steeper than the one through which you have just ridden. Cars far below look like toys, and small farmsteads quilt the valley in shades of green.

Gannett Hill takes its name from the first family to settle the area. Frank Gannett was born on a hill farm here in 1876; he went on to found what is today America's largest newspaper chain.

14.4 Turn LEFT at the T-junction onto Route 21 North (unsign-posted).

Route 21 gets some fast traffic; intermittently it has a ridable shoulder.

15.7 Just before reaching a small cemetery, turn RIGHT onto Bopple Hill Road.

Bopple Hill is very steep and although paved, it can be slippery with dirt and gravel. Old-timers tell of wagons loaded with grapes being skidded down Bopple Hill with their wheels locked—otherwise the wagons would have overrun the horses.

With wet or questionable brakes it would be safest to walk down Bopple Hill, or to follow the alternative route suggested below. If you decide to ride down the hill you should pull both brake levers with all your strength before starting down. If a cable is going to snap—and in time all cables do—you'll be safer if it breaks while you have both feet on the ground.

If you choose not to ride down Bopple Hill, simply continue north on Route 21 for about three miles and turn right onto Monks Road. In about a mile Monks Road ends at Seneca Point Road, where you should turn left to rejoin the tour route shortly before it crosses County Road 16.

Directly across the lake from Bopple Hill is Vine Valley, with Bare Hill to the north and South Hill, or The Whaleback, to the south. A Seneca Indian legend about Bare Hill is recounted in Tour # 5.

At lake level you'll find that Bopple Hill is now called Seneca Point Road. A mile and a half farther along, just before a long uphill, is Seneca Point, probably the most fashionable address on the lake. The summer colony here once included such well known New Yorkers as builder Robert Moses, New York *World* reporter Herbert Bayard Swope, and Thomas Fogarty, illustrator for *Cosmopolitan* and the *Saturday Evening Post*. Humphrey Bogart spent summers at Seneca Point as a child in his parents' cottage. Even Franklin Delano Roosevelt visited friends here in the 1920s.

After Seneca Point, the road climbs steeply and gradually for almost two miles.

19.9 Continue STRAIGHT at the Stop sign, crossing County Road 16.

If you look to the right at this intersection, you'll be looking down Miller's Hill.

21.7 Turn RIGHT at the Stop sign onto Route 21 North (unsignposted).

23.6 Another two miles brings you back to Cheshire, where the friendly dogs are probably waiting to announce your return.

Nearby bed and breakfasts include:
Nottingham Lodge B&B, 5741 Bristol Valley Road, Canandaigua, NY (716-374-5355)

Bicycle shops
Canandaigua Bicycle Center, 143 South Main Street, Canandaigua, NY (716-394-6150)
Sports Garden, Parkway Plaza, Canandaigua, NY (716-394-0644)

8

Naples—Honeoye Lake

31 miles; moderate cycling
Low rolling hills, with one steep section
County map: Ontario

Even though this tour goes for miles through wooded and farmed countryside and takes in only two small villages, it offers something for everyone, from the artist and theater-goer to the oenophile and gourmet. Except for a few miles bordering Honeoye Lake, most of the roads get very little traffic, although one should be alert on fine weekends in September and October when fall foliage lures tourists— many also to be enticed by autumn entrepreneurs selling Grandma's bustle, pictures of Great-Grandpa in his Civil War uniform, or genuine leaky wine casks. Naples also attracts visitors to view its vineyard-clad hills, tour the winery, hike trails to scenic overlooks, and fish its trout streams. Small galleries display the work of artists and craftspeople from the village and surrounding hills.

Honeoye, smaller than Naples and more influenced by plastics technology, would have disappeared altogether had the city of Rochester had its way in the 1930s and flooded the place for an enlarged reservoir. A visit to Sandy Bottom swimming beach near the village provides a view down the length of Honeoye Lake that will make you glad it's still as the glaciers left it. There are four nature reserves on or near this tour; one has a cafeteria and picnic tables, and at another is a well known "country gourmet" restaurant. You'll also pass near the Bristol Valley Playhouse, which has an active summer schedule.

The tour starts in Naples, located at the south end of Canandaigua Lake on Route 21.

0.0 Leave Naples' Main Street (Route 21) by going west on the unmarked street opposite Mechanic Street and the State

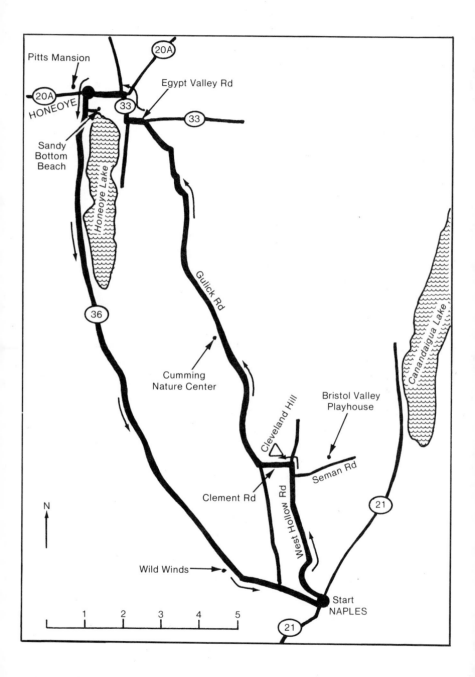

Pitts Mansion

20A

HONEOYE

Sandy
Bottom
Beach

20A

33

Egypt Valley Rd

33

Honeoye Lake

36

Gullick Rd

Cumming
Nature Center

Cleveland Hill

Bristol Valley
Playhouse

Seman Rd

Canandaigua Lake

Clement Rd

West Hollow Rd

21

N

Wild Winds

Start
NAPLES

21

1   2   3   4   5

Police office. This corner is just north of the main block of stores.

Aptly called by the Indians "The Place Between the Hills," Naples village is at the confluence of several glacial valleys. Grapes cover 1,200 acres in and around Naples, with eighty percent of them used in winemaking. Swiss-born John Jacob Widmer planted his first vineyard in 1883. It is located just west of the Widmer Winery Visitors' Chalet, and it still bears fruit. Free winery tours are offered from June 1 to October 31, noon to 4:30 p.m. on Sundays, and from 10:00 a.m. to 3:30 p.m. other days. The Widmer tour is among the most detailed offered by any winery; it is followed by a sit-down wine tasting.

Naples also has the 1794 Tellier House, adjoining a gift and antique shop at the north end of town, with the Old Village Square and pioneer cemetery directly across the street. Tellier House serves as the Naples Information Center. A little to the south, behind the modernistic Catholic Church, on Tobey Street, are displays of the Living Wall Garden, designed to grow flowers and vegetables using vertical rather than horizontal space. Economizing on land, water, and fertilizer, these gardens appeal to apartment dwellers and Middle East agricultural officials.

Fishing is popular along Naples Creek, said to be one of the most productive trout streams in the country. Over 6,000 people line the creek elbow-to-elbow on April 1, when the season opens with a one-day Trout Derby. Public fishing is also permitted at the bridge over Grimes Creek, at the end of Vine Street. It was in Grimes Glen that *Archeosigillaria primerum*, known as the "Naples Tree," was discovered in 1882. The thirty-three foot high fossil, now in the State Museum in Albany, provided the first evidence that trees as well as ferns grew in the Devonian period.

Bordering Naples on the east is the High Tor Wildlife Management Area, with nearly 6,000 acres for hunting, fishing, and hiking. High points overlook Canandaigua Lake and valleys south of it.

Naples restaurants include The Vineyard at the north end of town, the Naples Hotel in the center, and the Redwood at the southern extreme. There are restaurants in Honeoye as well, and each village has a supermarket.

0.1   Turn RIGHT onto Cross Street soon after passing the old mill. In 100 yards continue STRAIGHT through the intersection with Elizabeth Street, and begin the 700-foot climb out of town.

The uphill from Naples lasts for one-and-a-half miles and is a rugged way to begin a ride. However, this is the only stiff climb on the tour. Once out of town, Cross Street becomes West Hollow Road. Making your way slowly uphill, you may see kingbirds perched on utility lines. This robin-sized flycatcher is the only bird around with a white bar across the end of its tail.

When you've finished climbing, look back south toward Naples. You'll see a series of flat-topped hills all reaching about the same height. Geologists cite this as evidence that the region was once quite level, a peneplain later eroded by streams, then carved by glaciers, and now being down-cut by streams again.

The first road entering from the right after the climb is Seman Road. The modern hexagonal building about a mile up this road is the Bristol Valley Playhouse; here theatrical and musical performances are offered on summer weekends. Picnic tables are provided for pre-theater repasts. For performance schedules and ticket information call 716-374-6318.

About a half-mile past the Playhouse is the West Hill Nature Preserve, owned by the Nature Conservancy. On these 300-plus acres nature is being permitted to make the decisions on land once plowed and cleared by man.

3.9   Turn LEFT onto Clement Road. Here you will also be following signs to Camp Warren Cutler and the Nature Center.

The hill on your right is Cleveland Hill. A sign (perhaps hidden by weeds in summer) beside a dirt track locates the Bristol Hills Branch of the Finger Lakes Trail. There are good views from 2,000-foot-high Cleveland Hill. To the south the trail passes through Naples, then down Tannery Creek Gorge to High Tor. Maps of the Finger Lakes Trail can be obtained from FLTC, Inc., Box 18048, Twelve Corners Branch, Rochester, NY 14618.

4.7   At the T-junction turn RIGHT onto Gulick Road (unsignposted), again following the Nature Center sign. (Sections of Gulick Road may be patched and rough.)

At Wild Winds Farms flowers are used as garnishes for drinks and main dishes.

In a little under four miles you'll reach the entrance to the Cumming Nature Center, whose 819 acres are maintained by the Rochester Museum and Science Center. A new Visitors' Building has interpretive exhibits and a gift shop, plus a small cafeteria and restrooms. Picnic tables are nearby. In addition to several thematic nature trails, Cumming has developed a farmstead recreating the pioneer period of the 1790s, complete with a very popular team of oxen. Information on the frequently scheduled special programs can be had by calling 716-374-6160. Admission is $3 for adults, with reduced rates for senior citizens and children.

13.2 Bear LEFT at the fork, avoiding the road marked "No Outlet."

14.2 At the Stop sign turn LEFT onto Egypt Valley Road, County Road 33.

14.6 Turn RIGHT at the Stop sign, continuing on County Road 33.

15.2 Turn LEFT at the Stop sign onto Route 20A West.

On entering the village of Honeoye you may notice a motel whose name reminds visitors that they are on the route taken by the 1779 Sullivan Expedition, which sought to eliminate Indians from the region. The Sullivan Monument on the library lawn commemorates the erection of Fort Cummings here. The army sped its march toward the Genesee by leaving at the fort the "sick, lame and lazy," both equine and human.

The village of Honeoye, originally named Pittstown after its first settler, later took the more mellifluous name of its lake. This may seem an improvement—until one considers that the Indian word Honeoye means "a finger lying."

There are several restaurants and diners in the area, plus a grocery store.

16.0 Turn LEFT at the traffic light onto County Road 36.

For a short diversion, continue straight up the hill at this light for about 200 yards, where you'll see an historical marker identifying the Pitts Mansion, built in 1821 by Gideon Pitts, son of the area's first settler. Family sentiments supported abolition, and the house was a station on the underground railroad. Gideon's daughter, Helen, caused something of a stir in local and Washington society when she married the escaped slave and aboli-

tionist Frederick Douglass. Both are buried in Rochester's Mount Hope Cemetery. From the Pitts house, return
down the hill and turn right at the traffic light.

A half mile down County Road 36 you'll reach Sandy
Bottom Road, which leads to a fine swimming beach.
There is a picnic pavilion, and a lifeguard on duty from
noon to 7:00 p.m.

As you ride south toward the head of Honeoye Lake
(recall that all the Finger Lakes drain north) the hills on
either side of you heighten, but thanks to the cutting
power of the glaciers you will do little climbing. At the
head of the lake there is a good view of the wetlands
characteristic of the Finger Lakes' inlets. Sullivan's men
often complained of slogging through miles of "horrid
thick Mirey Swamp which render'd our proceeding ... difficult." South of the lake head the road undulates and
weaves pleasantly between hillside vineyards.

About twelve miles from Honeoye you'll reach Wild
Winds Farms, on your right. Begun in 1972 as an exper-
imental organic farm, Wild Winds has expanded to include a country store, gift shop, restaurant, and hiking and
cross-country skiing trails. Experiments in gardening and
viticulture are ongoing, and special attractions, from maple
sugaring to herb drying, vary with the season. The menus of
the justly praised gourmet restaurant range from moderately priced lunches served Tuesday through Sunday, to
$15 to $20 candlelight dinners served Friday and Saturday
(plus Thursday in July and August). If you arrive before meal
times you may see staff members in the gardens collecting
herbs and edible flowers with which the dishes are gar-
nished. Because the restaurant can be filled, reservations
for lunch and dinner are advised: call 716-374-5523. For
less elaborate eating, Wild Winds has a barbecue pavillion
with flower-decorated tables. Cafeteria-style lunches are
available here on Sunday in July and August. Fare such as
cold soups, steamed clams, and nitrite-free hotdogs is
served, along with some dishes form the fancier regular
luncheon menu.

After leaving Wild Winds, you'll pass through a pretty
bog favored by great blue herons.

30.9 Following a swoop downhill, you should be at the corner of Clark and Main Street in Naples, a few blocks south of your starting point.

Nearby bed-and-breakfasts include:
Billy's B&B, 4975 Bristol Valley Road, Honeoye, NY (716-229-2408)
The Greenwoods, 8136 Quayle Road, Honeoye, NY (716-229-2111)
Maxfield Inn B&B, 105 North Main Street, Naples, NY (716-374-2510)
The Vagabond Inn, 3300 Slitor Road, Naples, NY (716-554-6271)

Bicycle shops
Canandaigua Bicycle Center, 143 South Main Street, Canandaigua, NY (716-394-6150)
Park Avenue Bike Shop, 28 Lake Shore Drive, Canandaigua, NY (716-394-1530)

9

Canadice and Hemlock Lakes

29 miles; moderate to strenuous cycling
Rolling to hilly terrain
County maps: Livingston, Ontario

This tour circles the two most rustic of the Finger Lakes—the only ones with no cottages, marinas, restaurants, parks, or other development. Except for about four miles on state highways, riding is on back roads with little traffic. Sites of historic or cultural interest are few; this ride is largely for the pure pleasure of country riding in a sparsely settled countryside—occasionally it can seem eerily lonely. Toward the end of the tour a stop at a winery makes a pleasant return to "civilization." The most strenuous part of the tour involves a steep descent into the village of Springwater and an almost equally steep climb out again. Four miles are on unpaved roads, and elsewhere paving is sometimes rough.

The tour starts in the village of Hemlock, at the north end of Hemlock Lake.

0.0 Leave the village of Hemlock by riding south on Routes 15A and 20A. Continue STRAIGHT on route 15A just out of town as Route 20A goes to the left.

This quiet backwater was once a bustling area of three villages with lumber and flour mills, distilleries, and a potash factory. Hemlock village was known as Slab-City because settlers' houses were made of wood slabs. As this tour goes through a sparsely settled region, you should carry food with you. Hemlock has a small store, but it might be better to bring supplies from home.

Route 15A has a narrow-to-nonexistent shoulder and some fast truck traffic, but you ride it for only about a mile.

1.2 Turn LEFT onto Old Bald Hill Road.

2.9 Continue STRAIGHT, south, as you rejoin Route 15A. In two-tenth of a mile turn LEFT onto Coykendall (Hill) Road. Coykendall curves a lot but is easy to follow.

4.7   At the T-juncture, turn LEFT onto Purcell Hill Road.

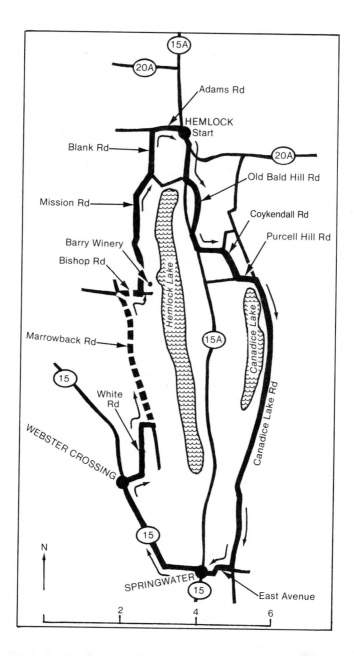

5.1   Turn RIGHT at the T-junction onto Canadice Lake Road.
We can only guess at the Indian sense of humor in naming the shortest of the Finger Lakes Shenadice, or "Long Lake." Three-mile-long Canadice is also the highest of the lakes, at 1,099' above sea level, and the most pristine in appearance—hardly an artifact of modern life is seen from its waters, and a scent of conifers along its shore enhances the feeling of being far from civilization.

A mile and eight-tenths along Canadice Lake Road you'll see a rutted dirt road to the right which gives access to the lake shore. You'll also see No Trespassing signs, intended to protect the lake from degredation, since Canadice, along with its neighbor Hemlock, is part of the city of Rochester's water supply system. Swimming is not permitted in the lake; fishing is allowed with a special free permit, used in conjunction with a regular state fishing license. Small boats, powerless or with motors up to seven horsepower, are allowed, again by special permit. Fishing and boating permits can be obtained by sending a stamped self-addressed envelope to Director of Water, 10 Felix Street, Rochester, NY 14608.

While Canadice and Hemlock Lakes look today somewhat as they must have before settlement by whites, it is surprising to learn that they were not always so. Actually, they have become progressively more rustic as the city of Rochester has gained more control over the watershed. The first water was piped north to the city in 1876, and a second conduit was built in 1893–94. Before that time Hemlock Lake had over a hundred cottages, five hotels, and five steamboats. The last of the cottages were removed shortly before World War II. Today Canadice and Hemlock supply about one-third of Rochester's water needs.

11.4 Continue STRAIGHT at the Stop sign at Wheaton Hill Road.
This is the second Stop sign at which you've continued straight. On the left after this one is the small Ford Cemetery. Toward the rear is the grave of a veteran of the Revolutionary War, one Pvt. Elisha Capron, once a soldier in Colonel Tupper's Massachusetts Regiment.

Two miles east of here is Tabor Hill (el. 2,244'), one of the highest points in the Finger Lakes.

12.7 Turn RIGHT at the Stop sign, onto East Avenue.

Before starting down the hill, look back north from this corner. The lake you see is Hemlock; Canadice is hidden to the right. Between them Bald Hill rises to 1,845 feet.

Caution is in order on the downhill that begins here, since it drops over 500 feet in less than one mile. The grade becomes more steep as you descend, and the paving becomes rutted—until it seems to disappear altogether. Dirt and gravel make the surface slippery. Sit well back on the saddle to get as much weight as possible over the rear wheel, which will discourage it from skidding. And don't hesitate to walk down if you doubt your brakes.

13.6 At the Stop sign at the bottom of the hill in Springwater, go STRAIGHT, following Route 15 North toward Livonia.

The valley village of Springwater has a grocery and luncheonette, antique shops, and a second-hand bookstore well known to area collectors. The climb from the village lasts about three-quarters of a mile. Riding Route 15 is unavoidable, but it does have a climbing lane for the hill and something of a shoulder thereafter.

17.2 In the hamlet of Webster Crossing, turn RIGHT onto May Road, opposite the church.

Webster Crossing has a general store and an outdoor pay phone. That's about it.

Canadice Lake is the highest and most rustic of the Finger Lakes. Because the lake is a reservoir for the city of Rochester, only small boats are allowed.

17.7 Turn LEFT with the road on which you've been riding, here called White Road.

19.1 Turn LEFT at the Stop sign, onto Marrowback Road. From here the road is unpaved for the next four miles.

Marrowback Hill reaches 1,940 feet, and the road is almost that high. The valley to the east contains Hemlock Lake, though the lake itself won't be visible for some time yet.

22.6 Turn RIGHT onto unsignposted Bishop Road. This is the first right turn possible; to the left at this intersection the road is marked for seasonal limited use.

23.2 Follow the road to the LEFT as it gradually becomes paved. (Do not enter the dead end straight ahead.) In two-tenths of a mile Vineyard Road, to the right, takes you to the Englecrest Vineyards.

The O-Neh-Da Vineyard was started on this site by Bishop Bernard McQuaid of Rochester in 1872 to make sacramental wine. The name comes from the Indian word for hemlock, and was their name for the lake. In 1924 it was purchased by the Society of the Divine Word, whose large seminary you'll pass about a half-mile north of the winery.

25.3 Keep RIGHT at the fork to enter Blank Road (unsignposted), which is briefly unpaved.

25.6 Continue STRAIGHT at the Stop sign. Here the road to the left is Town Line Road.

26.4 Continue STRAIGHT, crossing Harder Road.

27.2 At the askew T-junction, keep LEFT, on the paved road.

28.2 Turn RIGHT at the Stop sign onto Adams Road.

29.0 Turn RIGHT at the Stop sign onto Routes 15A and 20A. Soon you'll be back where this tour began.

Bicycle shops

Canandaigua Bicycle Center, 143 South Main Street, Canandaigua, NY (716-394-6150)

Ken's Cycle Shop, 53 Genesee Street, Avon, NY (716-226-2789)

Park Avenue Bike Shop, 28 Lake Shore Drive, Canandaigua, NY (716-394-1530)

Swain Ski & Sports, 131 Main Street, Geneseo, NY (716-243-0832)

10

Genesee Valley and Gorge

57 miles; easy to strenuous cycling
Varied terrain; flat stretches and both gradual and steep hills
County map: Livingston

One of the first Europeans to see the Genesee Valley described it as "the most beautiful flats I ever saw, being not less than 4 miles in width, and extending from right to left as far as can be seen." This tour passes through that valley and along the seventeen-mile length of the spectacular Genesee River Gorge in Letchworth State Park. Strong cyclists can do the ride in one day, though the first third of the ride is deceptively easy compared with the rest. Pushing to finish in one day would be a mistake for leisurely cyclists; and there's enough to see to repay fully spending two—or more—days on this route.

Overnight accommodations are available just short of the half way point at the Genesee Falls Inn in Portageville, which charges $30 to $39 for two. As there is no other place to stay in Portageville, reservations are suggested: call 716-493-2484. Overnight facilities in Letchworth State Park include tent and trailer campsites, log cabins, and inn accommodations. In summer Letchworth is very popular, and reservations are essential. Campsites and cabins can be reserved through Ticketron, or by writing or calling Letchworth State Park, Castile, NY 14427 (716-493-2611). To stay at the Park's Glen Iris Inn, write in care of the above address, or call 716-493-2622.

The tour starts at the intersection of Center and Main Streets in the village of Geneseo.

0.0   From the bear fountain, ride south on Main Street, so that the college and the Genesee Valley are to your right.

When the weary men of General Sullivan's 1779 expedition against the Iroquois finally saw the Genesee Valley, their farmers' eyes must have widened. Diaries acclaim, "a very beautiful flat of great extent growing up with grass higher than our heads ... the land can't be equalled ...

undoubtedly the best land, and capable of the greatest improvement, of any part of the possessions of the U. States."

The Genesee Valley did soon become the breadbasket of the nation, with Rochester the leading flour milling city

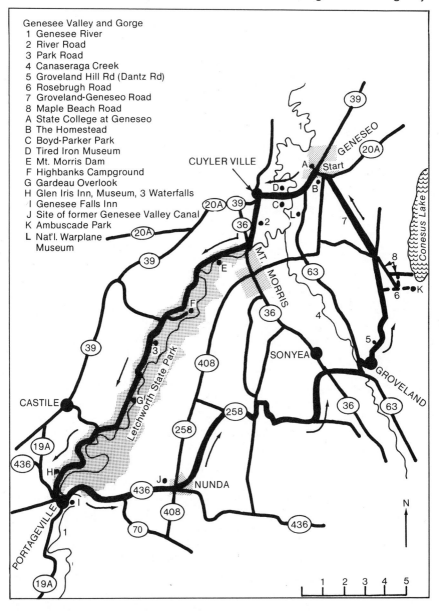

Genesee Valley and Gorge
1 Genesee River
2 River Road
3 Park Road
4 Canaseraga Creek
5 Groveland Hill Rd (Dantz Rd)
6 Rosebrugh Road
7 Groveland-Geneseo Road
8 Maple Beach Road
A State College at Geneseo
B The Homestead
C Boyd-Parker Park
D Tired Iron Museum
E Mt. Morris Dam
F Highbanks Campground
G Gardeau Overlook
H Glen Iris Inn, Museum, 3 Waterfalls
I Genesee Falls Inn
J Site of former Genesee Valley Canal
K Ambuscade Park
L Nat'l. Warplane Museum

in the world. Almost two hundred years after its sod first felt the plow, thousands of acres are still owned by the Wadsworth family, descendants of the first pioneers. Wadsworths have been farmers and congressmen, generals, senators, and ambassadors. Two branches of the family still live at either end of Geneseo's Main Street. In autumn the Wadsworth-initiated Genesee Valley Hunt rides cross-country after the fox.

W. Austin Wadsworth is one of the founders of the National Warplane Museum on the floor of the Genesee Valley, off Route 63. A few planes, including a World War II B-17 bomber, are on permanent display. But several dozen planes—landing, taking off, and flying in formation—can be seen at the remarkable September air shows. Museum hours are flexible. For details, write: National Warplane Museum, P.O. Box 5, Geneseo, NY 14454; or call 716-243-0690.

Since 1871 there has been a state college in Geneseo. The modern buildings of the State University College cling to the hillside, affording a grand view of the Genesee Valley.

Groceries can be bought in Geneseo and in most of the towns on this route; there is also a store in the Highbanks campsite of Letchworth Park.

0.3 Turn RIGHT at the Yield sign onto Routes 20A and 39. In 100 yards curve LEFT, following the sign to Dansville.

To your left are the grounds of the Wadsworth estate known as The Homestead.

1.3 Turn RIGHT, still following Routes 20A and 39 and a sign to Letchworth State Park.

In less than a mile you'll cross the Genesee River, and a mile beyond that you'll come to the Boyd-Parker Memorial Park. The park borders the site of a large Seneca Indian village called Genesee Castle, or Little Beard's Town. General Sullivan followed Washington's orders and destroyed the town; yet his official report sounds almost regretful: "The Castle consisted of 128 houses mostly large and elegant. The place was beautifully situated, almost encircled with a cleared flat, which extended for a number of miles, where the most extensive fields of corn were waving, and every kind of vegetable that can be conceived." The unlucky Thomas Boyd and Michael Parker, scouts sent out by Sullivan, were here tortured to death by their Indian captors on September 13, 1779. The next day Sullivan leveled the town, buried his men, and turned the army back east. They needed to go no farther; the Senecas had been destroyed.

The Boyd-Parker Park has picnic tables, rest rooms and pump water. Across the road is the Tired Iron Tractor Museum, where old farm machinery can be seen Sundays 11:00 a.m. to 6:00 p.m. May through October, admission $2.00.

3.7 Turn LEFT, following Routes 20A and 39 through Cuylerville.

3.9 Just after the fire house, turn LEFT onto River Road (unsignposted).

Flat, straight River Road parallels railroad tracks built on a filled section of the financially unsuccessful Genesee Valley Canal, begun in 1836, but abandoned in 1878.

6.1 Turn RIGHT at the Stop sign, and in fifty feet turn LEFT to enter Letchworth State Park.

In about two miles an overlook gives a spectacular view of the Mount Morris Dam and the almost 500-foot-deep canyon exposing some 400 millions years of geologic history. Park features include many overlooks of the river canyon, snack bars, restaurants, swimming pools, and hiking trails. About six miles into the park is the High-banks campsite, open from early May to early October.

Some five miles past Highbanks is the Gardeau Over-look, with an expansive view of lands once homesteaded by Mary Jemison, the "White Woman of the Genesee." As a girl Mary was adopted by Indians who killed the rest of her family in a frontier raid. For the next three-quarters of a century she lived as an Indian. She received title to more than 17,000 acres around Gardeau at the Treaty of Big Tree in 1797, where she acted as interpreter for the Indians. Thomas Morris, representing his father, Robert, was so worried that negotiations for Indian land would fall through without Mary's help, he agreed to give her the immensely valuable holding. The Treaty of Big Tree was finally signed by fifty-two Indians; among them were Hot Bread, Parrot Nose, and To-Destroy-a-Town.

22.7 Keep RIGHT at the fork, following signs to Upper Falls and Glen Iris.

In 1859 a rich bachelor named William Pryor Letchworth bought Glen Iris and a thousand acres around it as a summer retreat; for the next half-century preserving the whole Genesee Gorge, including the three fabulous waterfalls nearby, became his passion. The nucleus of the present park came into state ownership on Letchworth's death in 1910. The museum near the Glen Iris Inn has exhibits about Letchworth, Mary Jemison, and local Indian and pioneer history. The grave of Mary Jemison and a Seneca long house can be seen on the plateau above the museum. The Glen Iris Inn restaurant is open daily at meal times; guest rooms (within hearing distance of thundering Middle Falls) rent from $40 for a double, and are usually booked.

Geologists believe that the three great falls along this section of the river were formed as the ice sheet receded intermittently, lowering the water level and exposing new sections to downcutting. The 1852 railroad bridge over the Upper Falls was a major tourist attraction—the largest wooden bridge in the world—until it burned in 1875. In two months it was replaced by the iron bridge still standing.

25.0 Exit the park and turn LEFT at the Yield sign onto Routes 19A and 436.

25.3 Keep LEFT at the fork, following Route 436 toward Nunda.

25.7 At the Genesee Falls Inn, turn LEFT to follow Route 436 East across the Genesee River.

The Genesee Falls Inn is the only nineteenth-century tavern-inn remaining from the busy days of train excursions to see the wondrous bridge 250 feet above the raging river.

A steep climb of six-tenths of a mile brings you up the glacier-formed Valley Heads Moraine, stretching eastward across the whole Finger Lakes region, preventing the lakes from draining to the south. The moraine is also responsible for the Genesee Gorge; it blocked the Genesee River from its pre-glacial course, forcing it to excavate the gorge through what is now Letchworth Park.

28.6 Stay LEFT at the fork, following Route 436.

Two and a half miles farther, a sign on the left locates the lowest of seventeen locks which once carried the long-abandoned Genesee Valley Canal to Portageville over the hills you just coasted down. The locks can be seen best before foliage is fully out.

31.5 In the village of Nunda, turn LEFT onto State Street. In 200 feet, turn RIGHT onto East Street.

Nunda (Indian for "hill") has groceries and restaurants.

32.0 Turn LEFT at the Yield sign, and follow Walnut Street for about fifty feet; then turn RIGHT onto Creek Road.

36.1 Turn RIGHT at the Stop sign onto Route 258.

37.5 Turn LEFT at the Stop sign, following Route 258 East.

38.1 Still following Route 258 East, turn RIGHT.

41.2 Stay LEFT at the fork, to keep on Route 258.

43.9 Continue STRAIGHT at the Stop sign, crossing Route 36.

The wide valley you cross here holds only tiny Canaseraga Creek, which is much too small to have carved it. Geologists explain that the valley was formed by the Genesee River, which flowed here prior to the Ice Age. Today, the Genesee rejoins its old valley after emerging from the narrow Letchworth Gorge, near Mount Morris.

You may have noted that farmhouses over the last few miles often don't reflect the rich quality of the land. This is because many of the farms are owned by people living elsewhere and are leased to tenants. Livingston County has the highest proportion of tenant farms in the Finger Lakes.

45.8 Turn LEFT at the Stop sign, following Route 63 North toward Geneseo.

46.0 Just after the fire house, turn RIGHT onto the unsignposted road, following a small sign to Groveland Hill.

The Middle Falls of the Genesee River thunders through Letchworth Gorge near the Glen Iris Inn.

46.2 Turn LEFT onto Groveland Hill Road, also called Dantz Road.
This stiff uphill lasts over two miles, and brings you 750
feet above the valley.

Just over four miles from the last turn is unpaved
Rosebrugh Road. The direct route back to Geneseo continues straight, but to visit the site of the Groveland
Ambuscade, where Boyd and Parker were captured, turn
right here. In one and four-tenths miles a small Ambuscade sign points to the right, where you'll find a picnic
shelter and water pump. The memorial obelisk is reached
by a grass path from the uphill side of the park.

The Sullivan campaign was characterized by burned
Indian villages and crops, and few casualties on either
side. In terms of lives lost, the battle known as the Groveland Ambuscade was the most costly to the Colonials—
fourteen men were killed on the spot.

A lethal chain of coincidences began on the night of
September 12 when General Sullivan, who had only
sketchy maps, sent out a scouting party led by Sergeant
Thomas Boyd to locate a rich Indian town rumored to be
in the Genesee Valley. In darkness Boyd and two dozen
or so men crossed the Conesus Lake inlet, climbed
Groveland Hill and continued westward. They found only
a small abandoned village. At dawn the patrol turned back
east toward the main army, unaware that their path was
now blocked by a Tory-Indian force waiting in ambush on
Groveland Hill. The slaughter was quick and thorough;
only a few flankers escaped. But the firing on Boyd's
patrol alerted Sullivan to the enemy's presence. Having
lost the advantage of surprise, the Indians and British
retreated to Little Beard's Town, with Boyd and Parker as
captives. Though they had not intended to be martyrs, the
hapless scouting party saved the lives of many men in the
main force.

To continue toward Geneseo from the ambuscade site,
push back up the hill past Lakeview Cemetery, and turn
right at the corner onto the paved road (the less sharp
right turn). Keep going straight where you join Maple
Beach Road. In another mile, turn right at the Stop sign,
and then left at the fork, with Adamson's store to your right.

52.1 At the Stop sign, continue STRAIGHT for about 100 feet; then go LEFT at the fork, so that the abandoned store is to your right. This is Groveland-Geneseo Road.

56.5 In Geneseo, turn LEFT at the Stop sign, and RIGHT in thirty feet onto Temple Hill.

The brick Georgian mansion in the landscaped grounds to the left was built in 1827 by James Wadsworth as an academy, or high school. To staff it he hired three young Harvard graduates, one of whom, Cornelius C. Felton, was later president of that university.

56.7 Turn LEFT at the Stop sign onto Center Street. A half-mile of downhill coasting will bring you back where the ride began.

Those wanting to know more about local history can visit the Livingston County Historical Museum, at 30 Center Street. The museum, housed in an 1838 cobblestone school building, is open Thursday and Sunday 2:00 to 5:00 p.m., May through October.

Geneseo's famed Big Tree Inn is at 46 Main Street. The handsome 1833 Federal-style house was converted from private dwelling to inn by a Wadsworth scion in 1885. Today no lodging is offered, but gourmet lunches and dinners are served Monday through Saturday; an abundant "country breakfast buffet" is prepared 10:00 a.m. to 2:00 p.m. on Sunday. In the tap room food is available daily from 9:00 a.m. to 2:00 p.m. and 5:00 to 9:00 p.m. Dinners average about $15. The Big Tree's number is 716-243-2330.

Convenient overnight accommodations can be found across the street from the Big Tree, at American House Bed and Breakfast Inn, 39 Main Street. Rates start at about $45 for a double room (716-243-5483).

Nearby bed-and-breakfasts include:
Butternut B&B, 44 East Street, Nunda, NY (716-468-5074)
Conesus Lake B&B, 2388 E. Lake Road, Conesus, NY (716-346-6526)
MacPhail House B&B, 5477 Lakeville Road, Geneseo, NY (716-346-5600)
National Hotel B&B Inn, Route 20A, Leicester, NY (716-382-3130)
Oak Valley Inn, 4235 Lakeville Road, Geneseo, NY (716-243-5570)

Bicycle shops
Ken's Cycle Shop, 53 Genesee Street, Avon, NY (716-226-2789)
Swain Ski & Sports, 131 Main Street, Geneseo, NY (716-243-0832)

11

Pittsford—Erie Canal

19 miles; easy to moderate cycling
Flat canal towpath and low hilly terrain
County map: Monroe

Affluent suburbs often have a sameness that makes them hard to distinguish, and a blandness that makes the effort barely worthwhile. The Rochester suburb of Pittsford has its shopping center. But it also has some of the best old buildings in western New York, a quaint village center, working farms, and a restored towpath along the Barge Canal, which here follows the route of the original Erie. Pittsford antedates nearby Rochester by almost a quarter-century and has a long list of area firsts: saw mill, schoolhouse, library, post offices, newspaper. The Erie Canal enlivened Pittsford, but it created Rochester.

The significance of the Erie Canal is hard to appreciate today, when airplanes or the interstate highway system, for example, are mere supplements to other means of transportation. But for years the Erie was almost the only way through a wilderness scarred by scarcely a mud track. Men with shovels and wheelbarrows piled up dirt for four years to build the embankment you ride on between Bushnell's Basin and Pittsford. Over four miles of canal-side riding on the gravel towpath give level riding and a view you can imagine sharing with old-time "canawlers." Away from the towpath, the route winds through a region of working and genteel farms and passes through a vast county park with ponds for swimming or fishing. Convenient bike rentals are available from Sportecular and Towpath Bike Shop, both in Northfield Common, Pittsford.

The tour starts at Bushnell's Basin, on the Barge Canal some two miles southeast of Pittsford village, near the Bushnell's Basin exit of Route 490.

0.0 From the front of Richardson's Canal House, cross the bridge to the north side of the canal; then follow the towpath access path to the RIGHT. On the gravel towpath ride west, so that the canal is to your left.

Richardson's Canal House is perhaps the oldest canalside tavern surviving from the heyday of the old Erie Canal. Built in 1818 and first managed by brothers named Richardson, it was not a fancy inn; canalers came there to engage in drinking and brawling that soon became legendary, and to sleep on the floor. Today eight rooms accommodate guests and expertly prepared meals are served. An $8.00 buffet style lunch featuring homemade

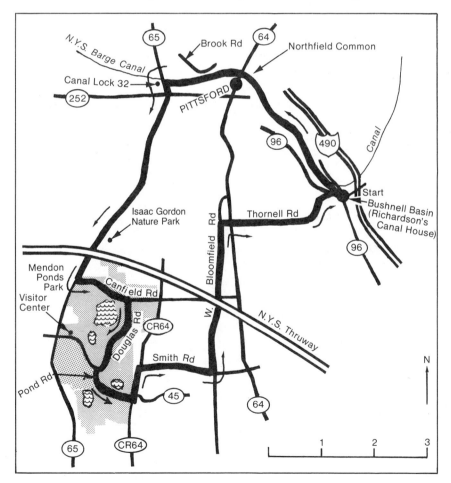

breads and patés, imaginative salads and relishes, and delectable desserts is served Monday through Friday 11:30 to 2:30. In good weather you can eat outside on the terrace and watch boats go by on the canal. Dinner is a fixed-price ($30.00), five-course feast with five entrees to choose from. The menu, a creative blend of Continental and American cuisines, changes monthly to take advantage of various fresh fruits and vegetables as they reach their peaks. Dinner reservations are advisable (716-248-5000).

From Bushnell's Basin to Pittsford village the canal is carried over the Irondequoit Valley on a man-made ridge called the Great Embankment. Heaping it up required a massive effort by men, mules and oxen. For two of the embankment's four construction years the great canal ended at the wide waters of Bushnell's Basin, and Richardson's (or simply the West End Tavern), was an especially busy place. As you might guess as you ride along the Great Embankment high above the surrounding countryside, a breach in the canal here could cause great damage. In the early years even so much as a muskrat burrowing in the earth banks could empty the canal and flood the neighborhood.

Those who want to carry food along can shop at the Hitching Post Plaza, across from the Canal House, or in Pittsford village, which also has several restaurants.

2.3 The towpath ascends to street level at the State Street Bridge. Cross State Street and enter the Northfield Common shopping area; take the LEFT fork to continue on the towpath.

Northfield's former industiral and warehouse buildings, once serving canal and railroad, were adapted to crafts shops, boutiques, and restaurants in the 1970s. This may be one of your few opportunities to eat in an old coal tower. There are also two bike shops, both of which have rentals.

For a diversion to see some of Pittsford village, ascend to street level and cross the bridge over the canal. A pleasant canalside part is to the left immediately across the bridge. Continuing straight, at the traffic light you'll see the old red brick Phoenix Hotel building. Now occupied by newspaper offices and several businesses, this harmonious Federal-style building dates from 1807, about twenty years after the first settlers arrived.

From the early days, Pittsford produced and attracted wealth with milling, farming, quarrying, small manufacturing, and legal, medical, and canal-related services; later, its charm and proximity to Rochester made it a choice for country estates. Some of Pittsford's best houses can be seen if you turn right, west, onto Monroe Avenue (Route 31), for a block or two. (It is best to walk on the sidewalk here, as traffic is often heavy.) The older buildings date from the late Federal period, roughly 1815 to 1830. The local historical society occupies the small former lawyer's office on the right. Other village streets are worth exploring, if you have time. A row of nineteenth century commercial buildings can be seen across Main Street from the Phoenix Building.

3.5 As the towpath is interrupted by a highway department garage, you must turn RIGHT. About 200 feet farther, turn LEFT onto Brook Road. In approximately another 200 yards, turn

Cyclists, joggers, and walkers enjoy miles of traffic-free quiet on the path beside the Erie Canal.

LEFT, following a sign for the Canal Park Trail.

4.3 At Lock 32, cross under the highway bridge and walk up the stairs, bordered by a ramp convenient for wheeling bicycles. From the canal park, turn RIGHT onto Route 65 South. (Care is needed in crossing the bridge over the canal, as there is no shoulder.)

>   From Lock 32, canal traffic going west has only one more lock to negotiate before entering the Long Level, sixty-three uninterrupted miles with "neither lock, block, nor stay to traffic" all the way to Lockport. In all, the present Barge Canal has thirty-five locks, less than half the number the Erie needed to bridge the 570-foot drop from Lake Erie to the Hudson River.

4.7 At the traffic light, go STRAIGHT across Route 252 to continue on Route 65 South.

>   The wide shoulder of Route 65 is marked as a bike path, and motor traffic should lessen as you proceed south. In about three miles, shortly before crossing over the New York State Thruway, you'll see the Isaac Gordon Nature Park on your left. A shaded main trail leads to two loops: the Hardwood Trail branches to the right, and the Pond Trail descends to the left. About a half-hour should be allowed for walking either trail; each has a picnic table.

8.5 At Canfield Road, turn LEFT into Mendon Ponds Park.

9.7 Turn RIGHT onto Douglas Road.

>   The ponds in this 550-acre park are excellent for swimming or fishing, and picnic tables, grills, and rest rooms are provided.

>   The park contains a variety of glacial features such as moraines, eskers, kames, and kettle holes. Diagrams and photos in the Mendon Ponds Visitor Center explain these interesting surface features and other aspects of local natural history. Self-guiding nature trails radiate from the center; feeding stations along them are usually successful in luring birds within easy view. The center is open 10:00 a.m. to 4:30 p.m. Wednesday through Sunday. To reach the center, do not exit the park as described below, but continue straight on Pond road for about a mile.

11.4 Leave the park by turning LEFT onto Pond Road.

12.2 Turn LEFT onto Mendon Center Road.

12.7 Make the first RIGHT turn possible, onto Smith Road.

14.1 Turn LEFT onto West Bloomfield Road.

17.0 Turn RIGHT onto Thornell Road.

Thornell Road is straight for a while, and then it twists as if designed by someone who hated cartographers. Despite the twists, clear signposting should allow you to stay on Thornell with little confusion.

19.4 At the stop sign, turn RIGHT onto Route 96 East. In a couple of hundred feet you'll be in sight of your starting place at Bushnell's Basin.

Nearby bed-and-breakfasts include:

Oliver Loud Tavern, 1474 Marsh Road, Pittsford, NY (716-248-5000)
Strawberry Castle, 1883 Penfield Road, Penfield, NY (716-385-3266)

Bicycle Shops

Recreational Vehicles & Equipment, 40 North Main Street, Fairport, NY (716-388-1350)
Spokes 'n' Wheels, 7374 Pittsford-Palmyra Road, Fairport, NY (716-223-4611)
The Ski Loft by Sportecular, 3 Schoen Place, Pittsford, NY (716-586-9390)
Towpath Bike Shop, 10 Schoen Place, Pittsford, NY (716-381-2808)

12

East Bloomfield—Powder Mills Park

32 miles; moderate cycling
Small hills with only a few level places
County maps: Monroe, Ontario

Although this route comes within seven miles of the Rochester city limits, it is a rural ride through attractive farm and woodland, with only eight-tenths of a mile unpaved. You'll visit a neat country village with an antique radio museum, pass an extensive orchard of easy-to-pick dwarf apple trees (bearing some of the largest apples you'll ever see), traverse a spacious county park with a trout hatchery, and stop at a comfortable rural restaurant beside a buffalo pasture!

In 1687, the Marquis de Denonville, then governor of New France with headquarters in Quebec, decided that the Indians had become "exalted to a tone of insolence that must be brought down." He was annoyed by their interference with the French fur trade and affronted at their resistance to French Jesuit missionaries. Attacking with 1500 Frenchmen and 500 Indian allies, Denonville wiped out four Seneca villages south and east of present-day Rochester. The sites of two of these villages are passed on this tour.

The ride starts at the green in the village of East Bloomfield, on Routes 5 and 20.

0.0 Begin by riding north (downhill) along the green's west side, the side facing the East Bloomfield Academy.

An 1845 newspaper advertisement for the East Bloomfield Academy promised instruction in English, Higher Mathematics, Greek, piano, French, German, practical surveying, and Civil Engineering. Today its handsome brick building houses the East Bloomfield Historical Society and the museum of the Antique Wireless Association, with displays that represent pioneering efforts in telegraph, telephone, phonograph, and television. A wall of the museum is stocked as a radio store would have been in 1925, when radio was a do-it-yourself hobby. No admission is charged, and the museum is open May 1 to October 31, Sunday from 2:00 to 5:00 p.m. and Wednes-

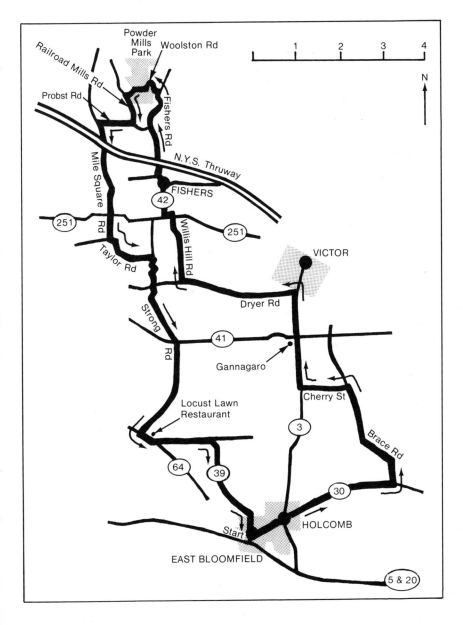

day 7:00 to 9:00 p.m. The Historical Society's side of the building is open from Memorial Day to Christmas, Wednesday through Saturday 1:00 to 4:00 p.m., plus the hours that the radio museum is open. To the left of the entrance you can find students' names incised in the brick facade along with nineteenth century dates—when, we can guess, the graffiti artists were hidden by shrubs.

Across Routes 5 and 20 from the Congregational church is Holloway House, a tavern and coaching inn dating from 1808. Another restaurant is passed near the end of the tour, but as no grocery stores are convenient, it is best to bring food with you.

0.1 Turn RIGHT at the Stop sign, to follow Route 20C east.

1.0 Go STRAIGHT at the traffic light, continuing on the street which becomes County Road 30 outside the village of Holcomb.

A historical marker on the left near Mud Creek commemorates the site of Gandagourae, a Seneca Indian village destroyed in the French raid. The Jesuits at the Saint Michel Mission here were recalled shortly before the raid was scheduled.

3.7 Turn LEFT onto Brace Road.

6.2 Turn LEFT onto Cherry Street.

7.3 At the Stop sign, turn RIGHT onto County Road 3.

In a short distance you'll pass Apple Farm, where in mid-May blossoms scent the breeze, and from late summer through October you can pick your own fresh apples. Throughout the year apples and snacks are for sale. Ironically, among the apple varieties grown here you will not find the Northern Spy, which was developed in an orchard on nearby Boughton Hill Road in 1800.

8.5 At the top of Boughton Hill, continue STRAIGHT at the flashing light.

Just before the intersection, a marker in the shape of a cross identifies the site of Gannagaro, once the Seneca capital, with perhaps 7,000 inhabitants. It was the summer of 1687 that Denonville marched on Gannagaro; his report summarized events: "On the next day, 14th July, we marched to one of the large villages where we encamped. We found it burned and a fort quite nigh; it was very advantageously situated on a hill. I deem it our best policy to employ ourselves laying waste the Indian corn which was in vast abundance in the fields, rather than follow a flying enemy to a distance and excite our troops to catch only some straggling fugitives." Though the French soon departed, Gannagaro was not reoccupied by the Indians; instead they drifted east toward Canandaigua and Geneva. The raid earned the French the lasting hatred of the Senecas, and led the whole Iroquois Confederacy to side with the English in the wars of the eighteenth century.

On the left, just after the intersection, is a good example of a house in the Italianate style, popular between 1840 and 1880, characterized by wide eaves supported by large brackets, tall windows, low-pitched hip roof, and double doors with glass panels. In 1986 this house, the nearby meeting house, and surrounding land were acquired by the Office of Parks, Recreation and Historic Preservation. Exhibits in the c. 1830 meeting house recount the story of early Indian settlement in the area.

9.4 Toward the bottom of the hill, Turn LEFT onto Dryer Road.

Two and a half miles farther, where Malone Road enters,

Cobblestone construction is indigenous to the northern Finger Lakes--Lake Ontario lowlands area.

are two good cobblestone buildings. The one closer to the road was built as a school in 1834.

12.2 Turn RIGHT at Willis Hill Road.

13.7 At the Stop sign, turn LEFT onto Route 251 for about 150 yards; then turn RIGHT onto County Road 42, following the sign to Fishers.

14.6 At the Yield sign, turn LEFT; cross the stream, and turn RIGHT onto Fishers Road.

For a look at the hamlet of Fishers (formerly Fishers Station, a stop on the Auburn and Rochester Railroad), turn right instead of left at the Yield sign. In a hundred or so yards on the right is a small cobblestone pump house. Built in 1845, it is said to be the second-oldest surviving railroad building in the country. (The oldest is in Baltimore.)

15.3 After passing under the New York State Thruway, stay to the RIGHT at the fork.

16.5 Where your road meets Benson Road, bend LEFT, staying on the paved Fishers Road, with the pond to your right.

16.8 Turn LEFT onto Woolston Road, following a sign to Powder Mills Park.

17.2 Continue STRAIGHT on Woolston Road, as a park road enters from the right.

The name Powder Mills recalls the gunpowder factories once here. The powder was shipped by wagon to Bushnell's Basin, there to be loaded aboard barges on the Erie Canal. Signs at this corner note various park attractions. To see the trout hatchery you turn right here; to fish for the trout continue straight, and in about a half-mile you'll come to a small stream stocked with trout—and fishermen. The 576-acre park is perfect for a lunch or refreshment break. It has picnic tables, drinking water, and rest rooms.

18.0 After following Woolston Road out of the park, make a LEFT turn of about 160 degrees onto Railroad Mills Road, which becomes unpaved in three-tenths of a mile and remains unpaved for eight-tenths.

18.9 At the T-junction, turn RIGHT onto Probst Road.

19.7 Turn LEFT at the Stop sign onto Mile Square Road.

22.3 Turn LEFT at the T-junction onto Taylor Road (unsignposted).

23.6 Turn RIGHT at the T-junction onto Strong Road.

Many of the small hills you ride over and around here are

kames, formed in temporary lakes created by glacial damming and melting. Streams flowing into the lakes carried the sand and gravel of which the kames are composed.

25.4 At the Stop sign, stay on Strong Road, which bends about twenty degrees to the right.

27.8 Turn LEFT at the Stop sign onto Route 64.

Before reaching this corner you'll pass the Locust Lawn, a moderately priced restaurant featuring ground beefsteak. Meals are served 8:00 to 11:00 a.m. and noon to 8:00 p.m. daily, except Monday. Across the road you may see bison, looking formidable but acting like contented cows. They are not for "beefalo" burgers; the owners of the Locus Lawn installed the herd only as a tourist attraction.

28.4 At the top of the hill, turn LEFT onto County Road 39.

29.8 As the road drops to a stream, stay on County Road 39, which here makes a ninety degree turn to the RIGHT. Do not cross the stream.

32.3 At the Stop sign, turn LEFT onto East Bloomfield's Main Street; in about fifty feet turn RIGHT, and you'll be facing the green where the tour began.

Nearby bed-and-breakfasts include:
Safari House B&B Deluxe, 950 Deer Crossing, Victor, NY (716-924-0250)
Woods Edge, 151 Bluhm Road, Fairport, NY (716-223-8877)

Bicycle shops
Canandaigua Bicycle Center, 143 South Main Street, Canandaigua, NY (716-394-6150)
Dixon's Bicycle Shop, 2174 Pond Road, Holcomb, NY (716-657-7871)
G.L. Keyes, 1309 Mertensia Road, Victor, NY (716-924-7282)
Park Avenue Bike Shop, 28 Lake Shore Drive, Canandaigua, NY (716-394-1530)
The Ski Loft by Sportecular, 3 Schoen Place, Pittsford, NY (716-586-9390)
Towpath Bike Shop, 10 Schoen Place, Pittsford, NY (716-381-2808)

13

Mormon Country

29 miles; moderate cycling
Low, rolling (drumlin) hills
County maps: Ontario, Wayne

Geologists come from far away to see the hills you'll be riding around and over on this tour. Between Lake Ontario and the Finger Lakes there are perhaps 10,000 drumlins—the largest such concentration in the world. Simply, drumlins are glacially formed hills shaped somewhat like an egg cut in half lengthwise. Generally less than 200 feet high, they are long from north to south, the direction of glacial flow, and steep and narrow from east to west. Cycling here you'll find that the vistas change constantly, as must your gear selection. After a few miles of east-west riding you'll likely have new respect for 200-foot-high hills.

One of the few drumlins with a name is Hill Cumorah, or Mormon Hill. It was here that Joseph Smith claimed to have received the golden plates of the Book of Mormon, sacred to the Church of Jesus Christ of Latter-day Saints. As geologists come for the drumlins, thousands of Mormons make pilgrimages to Hill Cumorah, Joseph Smith's home, the Sacred Grove, and Martin Harris' farm—all of which are passed on this tour. In addition, the ride passes the birthplace of modern spiritualism, a coverlet museum, and a canal park where you can see both the old Erie Canal and the modern Barge Canal. Fishing is possible along the route.

This ride does not begin near food stores, so you may want to bring supplies along with you. Both Palmyra and Newark along your route later on have groceries and restaurants.

The tour starts at the parking area of Hill Cumorah, on Route 21, four miles south of the village of Palmyra. (Note: during the Mormon Pageant, parking here is by permit only; then the tour can be started in Palmyra.)

0.0 From the parking area, ride south on Route 21, so that Hill Cumorah is to your left.

Hill Cumorah is a 683-foot-high drumlin; to its slopes the young Joseph Smith was directed by the Angel Moroni, son of Mormon, in 1823. Four years later, after presumably proving worthy, he was allowed to remove the golden plates containing the Book of Mormon from the hill and was inspired with the ability to translate the unknown language in which they were written. According to the Mormons, Hill Cumorah was the site of a fatal battle between peoples called Nephites and Lamanites in A.D. 420. The Hill Cumorah Pageant, held each year toward the end of July, recounts this conflict, as well as other

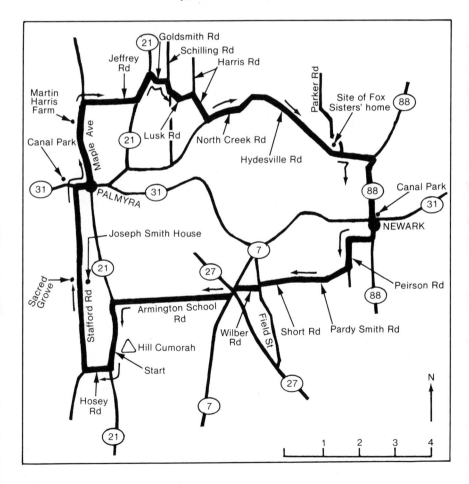

events important in Mormon legend. The outdoor performances start at 9:00 p.m. and admission is free. For details call 315-597-5851.

0.5   Turn RIGHT onto Hosey Road.

1.2   At the T-junction, turn RIGHT onto Stafford Road.

Here riding is between long, low drumlins—much easier than riding east-west over them.

In about two and a half miles you'll come to the Joseph Smith Farm. The house was started by the Smiths in 1822 and occupied by Joseph, his parents, and his seven siblings from 1825 to 1828. Some of the Book of Mormon was translated here. Apart from this historic connection, the house has interesting period furnishings and implements. Tours are free; some proselytizing may be encountered.

Across the road from the house is what Mormons call the Sacred Grove, where, in 1820, Joseph Smith is supposed to have first seen the Angel Moroni. Yearly meetings followed each September from 1823 to 1827, when the golden plates were entrusted to Smith. The Sacred Grove and the path to it are nicely landscaped and quite pretty.

5.6   At the intersection with Route 31, Main Street, turn RIGHT (east).

If you ride west instead for about a quarter-mile, you can visit the largest canal park along the state's waterway system, with picnic tables, rest rooms, and drinking water. This is also the most convenient place to compare the old Erie Canal with its modern Barge Canal successor; standing in one spot, you can watch boats passing through Lock 29 and see an aqueduct built in 1856 that once carried the Erie over Ganargua (Mud) Creek. The creek is a popular local fishing spot.

6.0   At the corner with the four churches, turn LEFT onto Maple Avenue, here called Canandaigua Street.

If you continue straight on Main Street into Palmyra village, noted for its Victorian architecture and cast iron store fronts, you'll find groceries and restaurants.

Henry Wells, co-founder of Wells-Fargo Express Company, started his business in Palmyra, delivering small packages on foot in the early 1840s. North of Main Street, at 122 William Street, is the Alling Coverlet Museum, housing the largest collection of coverlets in the country. May through October the museum is open 1:00 p.m. to 4:00 p.m. Admission is free.

Palmyra was one of the first towns settled in Wayne County (1789), but it did not flourish until the building of the Erie Canal in the 1820s. This period in its history is treated in the novel *Canal Town* by Samuel Hopkins Adams. Each September, Palmyra celebrates its historic relationship with the canal with a long weekend of events called Canaltown Days; for a schedule write to: Palmyra Canaltown Days, P.O. Box 64, Palmyra, NY 14522.

A mile and a half down Maple Avenue is a cobblestone house on the Martin Harris Farm. Harris was intrigued by Joseph Smith's translating of the Book of Mormon; eventually he mortgaged his farm to pay for its first printing. Harris' wife remained skeptical, however, and she purloined 116 pages of Smith's translation. This section was never re-translated. The unbelieving Mrs. Harris moved to her half of the farm, and Martin Harris eventually lost his.

The handsome cobblestone house post-dates Harris' ownership, though the well in front of it is believed to have been dug by Joseph Smith's father and brother. Inside, the house is modern, with displays telling the Mormon version of Harris' story.

Past the Harris farm, the railroad tracks at the bottom of the hill are rather bumpy.

8.1   Soon after Center Road enters from the left, turn RIGHT onto Jeffrey Road.

Here you begin riding up and down the steep east and west sides of drumlins.

9.5   At the Stop sign, turn LEFT onto Route 21 North.

10.4 Turn RIGHT onto Goldsmith Road.

11.1 Keep RIGHT at the fork, which brings you up to Shilling (sometimes spelled Schilling) Road heading south.

11.4 Turn LEFT onto Lusk Road.

12.1 At the T-junction, turn RIGHT onto Harris Road.

12.7 Turn LEFT at the Stop sign onto North Creek Road, County Road 223.

13.6 Follow the road to the LEFT, uphill, after passing a turnoff to Whitbeck Road. At the top of the hill, continue STRAIGHT; do not take Lyon Road.

14.0 Turn RIGHT at the Stop sign onto Hydesville Road, County Road 221.

Just under three miles farther, at Parker Road, on the left is a site associated with one of the quasi-religious movements of the nineteenth century which earned the area the sobriquet "burned-over district." Here lived the Fox sisters, founders of modern spiritualism. The "Hydesville rappings" began in 1848 when two of the Fox girls, Margaret and Catherine, reported strange knocking. The teenage girls soon invented a code to communicate with the source of the sounds, claiming that it was the uneasy spirit of a peddler murdered in the house some years before. There were skeptics, but also a surprising number of believers. Soon the girls were holding seances in nearby Rochester. With an older sister as publicist and booking agent, the Fox sisters were soon among the most famous people in pre-Civil War America. Séances were held for U.S. Senators and such notables as Horace Greeley, James Fenimore Cooper, William Cullen Bryant, George Ripley, and the wife of President Franklin Pierce.

After decades of travel, fame and infamy, adulation and

Joseph Smith's home is one of the sites near Palmyra associated with the founding of the Mormon Church.

scorn, wealth and scrimping, Margaret Fox admitted that the early Hydesville rappings had been produced with an apple on a string. Later the girls learned to make a suitable sound by cracking a joint in the foot, which made their act portable. In 1888, in a speech at the Academy of Music in Brooklyn, New York, Margaret Fox apologized for the "horrible deception." Despite that, the Fox Sisters' brand of spiritualism has adherents today.

17.7 Turn RIGHT at the Stop sign onto Route 88 South.

In just under a mile and a half, Newark Canal County Park to the left borders the Barge Canal, and has a picnic area.

19.5 After passing the center of Newark, turn RIGHT onto High Street, opposite the village green.

19.7 Turn LEFT at the Stop sign onto Mason Street.

On the right at this intersection is the Newark Public Library, which houses the Hoffman Clock Museum. Its antique timepieces can be seen during library hours. Admission is free.

20.0 At the Stop sign, turn RIGHT on to West Maple Avenue.

20.4 Turn LEFT at the Stop sign onto Peirson Avenue.

21.1 Turn RIGHT onto Pardy Smith Road.

22.5 At the T-junction, turn RIGHT onto Turner Road, and in 150 yards, turn LEFT onto Short Road.

23.6 At the T-junction, turn LEFT onto Field Street, and in 150 yards, turn RIGHT onto Wilber Road.

24.3 Turn LEFT at the T-junction onto County Road 7.

24.5 Pass the intersection with County Road 27, and 100 yards farther turn RIGHT onto Armington School Road.

27.5 Turn LEFT onto Route 21 South. In just over a mile you'll be back at Hill Cumorah. (If you have energy left, the paved road to the top of the hill is six-tenths of a mile long.)

Nearby bed-and-breakfasts include:

Canaltown B&B, 119 Canandaigua Street, Palmyra, NY (315-597-5553)

Bicycle shop

Park Avenue Bike Shop, 28 Lake Shore Drive, Canandaigua, NY (716-394-1530)

14

Lake Ontario Shores

40 miles; easy cycling
Mostly level terrain with some low hills
County map: Wayne

This Wayne County route takes the cyclist along roads bordered by orchards, orchards, and more orchards. From mid-May flowering to autumn maturity a scene of bucolic order pleases the eye, as rows of carefullly tended fruit trees pattern lowlands and gentle rises. It will come as no surprise that Wayne County ranks first in the state in apple production and is fourth in sour cherries; peaches, plums, apricots, and pears complete the county-wide fruit salad.

The fruit orchards are here because of Lake Ontario's moderating influence on the weather; and the lake is also indirectly responsible for the large number of cobblestone houses. This masonry is unique to the region south of the lake, cobbles having been formed in former lakebeds and along earlier shorelines. The first cobblestone houses were built in the area some time around 1825, probably by masons who had worked on the Erie Canal locks. A high quality of craftsmanship, and care in selection of stones depending on size, shape, and color, produced many houses of distinction. The Lake Ontario lowland and northern Finger Lakes areas have some 800 cobblestone houses extant; Wayne County leads all others with about 175. Over twenty such buildings are seen along this route.

The lake makes one more contribution to the appeal of this tour: both Ridge Road and Lake Road, one following a former and the other the present shore line, provide miles of level cycling; a major east-west highway running between the two draws off most of the through traffic. There are opportunities for swimming and fishing on this excursion as well as several attractive B & B's near Sodus Point.

Begin the ride at the tip of Sodus Point, on the west side of

Sodus Bay. As the area is residential, it is best to leave your car near the commercial section of Bay Street, and cycle to the end of the peninsula.

0.0   From the tip of Sodus Bay you can ride in only one direction, west, along Bay Street.

The spit of land which forms Bay Street, along with other bars and islands, gives Sodus Bay outstanding natural protection from Lake Ontario storms. Captain Charles Williamson, in charge of developing much of western New York for the English Pulteney interests during the last decade of the eighteenth century, considered it "the best harbour on the south side of Lake Ontario. Few or none, even on the seacoast, exceed it for spaciousness and beauty."

Though it flourished briefly, the town on the bay did not live up to the expectations of early speculators. Burned to the ground by the British during the War of 1812, it suffered further setbacks as a port after the completion of the Erie Canal in 1825.

Also in the nineteenth century, railroad tycoon Edward H. Harriman had grandiose plans for development; little remains of these designs except Margaretta Grove, a small park given to the town by Mrs. Harriman, which you'll pass on your way out of the village.

Today Sodus Point is largely a summer playground for fishing and boating; sailing is particularly popular in the sheltered waters. Along the north shore of the town, Sodus Point Park has picnic facilities and a bathhouse for

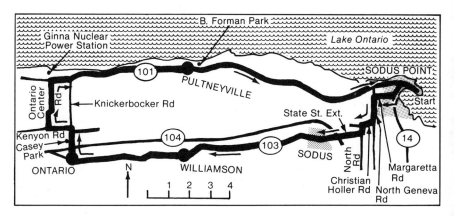

swimmers. There are several small restaurants and groceries along Bay Street. Similar-sized businesses appear
in most of the villages along the route, with one large
restaurant near the end of the tour.

A right turn onto Ontario Street (the last house on the right
before this turn once belonged to the Harrimans) leads
toward the lake and Big Sodus Light, restored and maintained by the Sodus Bay Historical Society. The first light-
house on this site was built in 1825 and was replaced by the
present structure in 1871. The lighthouse-museum is open
Saturday and Sunday 1:00 to 5:00 p.m. South of the light-
house, what had once been the installation's carriage
house has been adapted for use as guest rooms by the
Carriage House Inn.

1.0   Turn LEFT at the Stop sign onto Route 14, Fitzhugh Street.

1.6   Just before Margaretta Grove Park, turn RIGHT onto Margaretta Road.

2.7   Turn LEFT at the Stop sign, onto North Geneva Road, County
Road 140.

3.9   Turn RIGHT onto Christian Holler Road.

The road's unusual name is said to come from an odd, and
presumably noisy, sect of Christian fatalists who predicted
the world would end in 1823.

4.5   Turn LEFT onto North Road.

4.8   Turn RIGHT onto State Street Extension.

The orchards which you have begun riding through will
continue with few interruptions until you are back at
Sodus Point. One reason for good fruit production is that
Lake Ontario retards the season a bit, providing a cool
spring and some protection from early autumn frosts; thus
buds are less likely to be nipped by a May freeze, and fruit
can be harvested into October.

6.2   At the intersection with Route 104, continue STRAIGHT.

6.8   Again, continue STRAIGHT at the traffic light.

Sodus has long been the site of fruit processing plants
and, in the 1880s, it led the nation in apple drying. Sodus
earlier made attempts to start a silk business, which an
1838 newspaper declared was "... as simple as feeding
pigs and very easy to perform, one in which small children
could be made useful, and also decayed widows and
decrepit females ..." But the mulberry trees did not thrive
and the industry died.

A major fire gutted downtown Sodus after the turn of the century; the rebuilding was not very successful, and the town does not reflect the bountiful aspect of its countryside.

7.2 Continue STRAIGHT as Route 88 merges with Sodus' Main Street.

7.7 Turn LEFT onto Ridge Road, County Road 103; do not continue to the junction with Route 104.

The Ridge Road follows a low rise marking a former shore line of a larger precursor to Lake Ontario which geologists call glacial Lake Iroquois. As you ride, the land to your right was once lake bottom. The ridge served as a natural highway for soldiers and early settlers, and later it supported a Rochester-to-Sodus Point trolley with spring excursions advertised as "forty miles of blossoms." The ridge was also an easily accessible source of fine, water-smoothed cobblestones for house construction.

Cobblestone construction started as a simple, cheap expedient for farm buildings, but it quickly became popular with people who could afford to build with other materials. Though all cobblestones result from glacial action, they are divided into two types—ice-laid, or field cobbles, and water-laid, if they received a final tumbling and smoothing in stream or lake after being released from the ice. Water-laid cobbles are smaller, smoother, and rounder than field cobbles; they were suited for delicate designs or patterns and were often used for the fronts of houses, while field cobbles were relegated to side and rear sections. Since cobblestone construction peaked in the 1830s and 40s, most houses are in the Greek Revival style then popular, though a few Gothic Revival or Italianate homes survive. You'll count nearly two dozen cobblestone structures along this route; many are on the ridge itself.

12.5 Keep LEFT at the fork, staying on the Ridge Road, not Old Ridge Road.

In this area you may notice a derelict windmill and many Dutch names on mailboxes. East Williamson is still predominantly Dutch, populated by descendants of settlers who arrived between 1840 and 1845.

13.7 In the village of Williamson continue STRAIGHT at the traffic light, crossing Route 21.

Williamson considers itself the fruit capital of the county

Goats are less common than cows, and are much better climbers.

and annually celebrates Apple Blossom Time, a week-long festival in mid-May. Cycling at that time of year, you'll pedal among a profusion of blossoms.

Just outside of Williamson, there's a cobblestone building converted for use as a gas station. It is only in the last two decades that cobblestone structures have been treated as historic landmarks, and some still serve mundane purposes.

18.7 Continue STRAIGHT at the traffic light in the village of Ontario.

Ontario has small luncheonettes and natural foods grocery.

18.9 Turn RIGHT onto Knickerbocker Road, County Road 108.

19.3 Go STRAIGHT at the Stop sign, crossing Route 104.

Just over half a mile farther is the entrance to Casey Park, which occupies the site of a former surface iron ore mine. A Mr. Knickerbocker discovered the ore deposit in 1811, and mining and smelting were important local industries in the nineteenth century. Activity peaked in the 1880s, then declined rapidly after the discovery of the rich Mesabi Range in Minnesota. Small workings to supply dye to makers of red barn paint continued through the 1940s. A mile-long excavation is filled with spring water and makes a fine swimming site. The bordering parallel ridges are mine tailings. A map in the park points out other area landmarks connected with the mine.

20.1 Turn LEFT on Kenyon Road.

A couple of hundred yards along on the right, you may see a goat farm, with inquisitive goats jostling each other along the fence, looking for a handout or a pat on the head.

21.1 Turn RIGHT at the Stop sign at the first intersection onto Ontario Center Road (unsignposted).

A mile farther, at the Brick Church Road crossing, is Heritage Square, which preserves a log cabin and a one-room school. May through September it is open weekends, 1:30 p.m. to 5:00 p.m., although the working pump can be used to fill water bottles at any time.

23.5 At the Stop sign, turn RIGHT onto Lake Road, County Road 101.

Across the road, behind the innocuous Ginna Training Center sign, is the Ginna Nuclear Power Station of

Rochester Gas and Electric. Ginna made headlines in January of 1982 when it vented radioactivity into the atmosphere. The company formerly had public tours of the facility, but these have been cancelled.

You'll have your first good view of Lake Ontario shortly, with opportunities for fishing at the boat launching sites.

29.6 At the Stop sign in Pulteneyville, continue on Lake Road as it turns about 30 degrees to the LEFT; do not take the sharp left turn.

Pulteneyville is finely preserved, with grand old houses fortunate to have owners with the will and ability to keep them up. Rochester journalist Arch Merrill is not guilty of much hyperbole in writing, "Pulteneyville is a dream village, a bit of old New England's shore—without the stern and rock-bound coast—and in a fairer, greener land." Pulteneyville was a thriving village of ships' captains, many from New England, who preferred to live in sight of water in houses of familiar style. By the time lake shipping and ocean whaling declined, rich Rochester people were ready to take the captains' houses for summer or year-round residences.

A monument by the shore recalls the captains and ships of Pulteneyville's booming years of sail. Another recounts the defense of the town against British forces during the War of 1812. Local men did gather hastily under General Swift on May 15, 1814; the plaque omits to mention that they surrendered the next day.

Less than a mile past Pulteneyville is B. Forman Park, with picnic tables, rest rooms, and drinking water. This originated as Camp Forman, a recreation area for employees of the Rochester-based apparel firm.

About four miles farther, Cinelli's Country House Restaurant sits amid meticulous lawns overlooking acres of orchards. An anomaly in this rural fruitland, Cinelli's draws distant urbanites to sample the homemade Italian specialties. The restaurant serves Tuesday through Friday noon to 2:00 p.m., and 5:00 p.m. to 9:00 p.m.; Saturday 5:00 p.m. to 10:00 p.m.; and Sunday 1:00 p.m. to 8:00 p.m.

Less than two miles from Sodus Point you'll pass the Maxwell Creek Inn, on the left. Room rates in this large 1840 cobblestone inn start at $35 (315-483-2222).

40.3 Go STRAIGHT at the Stop sign onto Bay Street, leading back to where the tour began at Sodus Bay, which Williamson, ever the promoter, proclaimed "one of the most magnificent landscapes the human fancy can picture."

Nearby bed-and-breakfasts include:
Carriage House Inn, 8375 Wickham Boulevard, Sodus Point, NY (315-483-2100)
The Corner House, 8415 Bay Street, Sodus Point, NY (315-483-6700)
Maxwell Creek Inn, 7563 Lake Road, Sodus, NY (315-483-2222)
Silver Waters Guest House, 8420 Bay Street, Sodus Point, NY (315-483-8098)

Bicycle shops
Spokes 'n' Wheels, 7374 Pittsford-Palmyra Road, Fairport, NY (716-223-4611)
Western Auto, 16-18 West Main Street, Sodus, NY (315-483-6251)

15

Montezuma Marsh

38 miles; moderate cycling
Many low hills and some level stretches
County maps: Seneca, Wayne

Few people ever said the Montezuma Marsh was beautiful. Except for itinerant outlaws, it had few human inhabitants with the means to get away. It bred mosquitoes and other noisome bugs; it exuded what in the last century was believed to be "bad air," known now as malaria; it mired wagons; it was not good for corn, wheat, or cattle; and it made construction of the Erie Canal almost impossible.

But if you could get the opinion of birds—especially of geese and ducks—you'd get another picture altogether. A fine place, they might say, with water to swim in, weeds to eat, muck and quicksand to discourage predators. Human perceptions differing so radically from avian ones, it is understandable that the Montezuma Marsh was almost drained dry in the early years of this century, and that it did not become a National Wildlife Refuge until 1938. Since then, bird and bird-fancier have delighted in Montezuma, especially during spring and fall migration seasons. As this tour begins at Montezuma, an early start can get you there while the mist is rising and the geese, herons, coots, muskrats, and deer are breakfasting placidly. The four-mile-long gravel road through the refuge is well-graded and little used.

You'll border or cross several waterways along this route, some natural, some manmade. Though the old Erie Canal, completed in 1825, is virtually gone, you can explore its best-preserved relics at the Lock Berlin Canal Park. The 1918 Barge Canal uses sections of the old Erie and parts of natural rivers and lakes. (The Erie had to be wholly manmade in order to control water level through flood and drought.) The Barge Canal today caters mostly to pleasure craft, and you pass an operating lock along this route. East of Montezuma

Marsh you'll see the Cayuga and Seneca Canal, linking the two longest Finger Lakes to the Barge Canal system.

There are no concessions in or near the refuge, so you may want to bring food with you. The village of Clyde, about a third of the way through the route, has a grocery store and a couple of restaurants.

The tour starts in the parking area of the Montezuma National Wildlife Refuge, off Routes 5 and 20, three miles east of Seneca Falls. The first four miles are on unpaved Refuge roads.

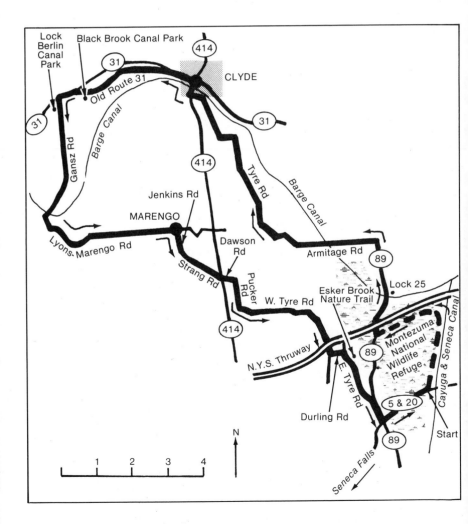

0.0   From the parking area by the visitors' center, follow the gravel road north into the wildlife refuge.

At the visitors' center are displays of stuffed birds, maps, and useful explanatory pamphlets. There is also a clipboard for recording recent bird sightings, and details on refuge areas temporarily closed to visitors. To see birds and other wildlife it is best to start riding as soon after dawn as possible, ideally on a weekday.

Montezuma National Wildlife Refuge's approximately ten square miles of wetland and field are visited by thousands of waterfowl traveling the Atlantic Flyway. In April and October, migrating geese and ducks number about 150,000. Little can compare to the thrill of seeing— and hearing—thousands of Canada geese leaving the refuge in the morning or returning at dusk. At peak times you can see phalanxes of geese in every quadrant of the sky. Warblers are common in May and June, and many other birds and mammals, including deer, are seen throughout the year. Since 1976 a program to re-establish bald eagles in New York has used Montezuma as a hacking site, so it is possible to see one of these extremely rare birds flying free. Warm water fish, particularly the bullhead, northern pike, and walleye, draw anglers to the waters bordering the refuge.

Before the swamp was drained in 1911, Montezuma Marsh was twelve miles long and eight miles wide, one of the largest freshwater marshes in North America. With contiguous Cayuga Lake it was a formidable barrier to east-west travel. In *The Erie Canal*, Ralph Andrist recounts that for diggers of the canal, relief at the easy shoveling was short-lived: cuttings oozed full of mud, quicksand swallowed retaining walls, leeches and mosquitoes attacked; in 1819 over a thousand men died of malaria at Montezuma. A harried doctor by chance tried a new drug from Peru, which happened to contain quinine. The canal was dug; but not before the men had added a new verse to their ballad of woes:

> *We are digging the Ditch through the mire;*
> *Through the mud and the slime and the mire, by heck!*
> *And the mud is our principal hire;*
> *In our pants, up our sleeves, down our neck, by heck!*
> *The mud is our principal hire.*

3.9 After following the gravel refuge road north and then west, parallel to the New York State Thruway, turn RIGHT at the Stop sign onto Route 89 North.

A mile along you'll pass over the Barge Canal, with Lock 25 to the right. If you're lucky, a boat may be "locking through." For a closer view you can turn right onto May's Point Road before reaching the bridge. The road dead-ends at a small canal park; the detour totals seven-tenths of a mile.

6.7 Turn LEFT onto Armitage Road. At this intersection Wayne County begins and Route 89 turns right.

Beside Armitage Road, lowlands are diked and drained by gravity and pumps so that potatoes and celery can be raised on the rich, heavy muckland soil.

At the Galen town line, Armitage Road becomes Tyre Road.

10.1 At the Stop sign, turn RIGHT on the unsignposted road; this is still Tyre Road, County Road 372.

12.7 Turn LEFT at the T-junction.

14.4 On the outskirts of Clyde, turn LEFT onto Redfield Street.

14.6 Turn RIGHT at the Stop sign, taking Mill Street over the Clyde River.

Here the river carries Barge Canal traffic; the old Erie ran a few rods south of the river.

15.0 In the center of the village of Clyde, turn LEFT on North Park Street. At the far side of the village green, turn LEFT and immediately RIGHT, to follow Route 31 West, West Genesee Street.

Clyde was named for the Scottish river in 1818, and its main thoroughfare is Glasgow Street; yet this canal town has had a large Italian community since the 1860s when immigrant labor was needed for railroad construction, and later for widening the Erie Canal. The statue of George Washington on the village green was erected during World War II by the Sons of Italy to allay suspicions about their allegiance.

A pioneer glass factory, in operation here until 1912, developed the Mason type fruit jar. The Galen Historical Society Museum on Sodus Street features a Clyde glass exhibit; it is open weekends 2:00 to 4:00 p.m. in June, July, and August.

16.2 Turn LEFT onto the unsignposted road branching from Route

31 opposite a Sunoco station.

This narrow road, rough in parts, is Old Route 31. A relic from the days of smaller and slower cars, it gets little traffic.

Two and a third miles farther is Black Brook Canal Park, with picnic tables and a covered shelter, rest rooms, and drinking water. A path from the right side of the picnic shelter leads, in about a hundred feet, to the original Erie Canal, where a grassy track follows the old towpath. Canal buffs may want to walk the eight-tenths of a mile to Lock Berlin, to rejoin the cycling route there. If so, walk west on the towpath.

18.8 Turn LEFT at the Stop sign onto Route 31 West.

19.3 Turn LEFT beside the hamlet of Lock Berlin, following a sign to the Canal Park (Gansz Road).

Lock Berlin Canal Park has picnic tables, rest rooms, and cold well water. But the real attraction is the finest set of locks remaining from the Erie Canal. If the gate is unlocked,

The double locks at Lock Berlin Canal Park are the best set surviving from the old Erie Canal.

a small bridge allows you to reach an artificial island between the locks to examine every scratch and rope-worn stone in detail.

Legend and folklore have embellished the romance of the old canal; yet exaggerating its importance would be difficult. Before it was built, the longest canal in America was the twenty-seven-mile-long Middlesex Canal in Massachusetts; the Erie was to cross 363 miles of wilderness, and need 83 locks. Even the perspicacious Thomas Jefferson, while admitting the canal was a good idea, declared that it was a century too soon, and "little short of madness to think of at this day." For once, Jefferson was wrong; in 1817 New York State forged ahead. In October of 1825 the Erie was completed. The Middle West was opened to rapid settlement, farmers gained access to distant markets, and cities from Buffalo to New York sprang up like mushrooms and prospered.

Lock Berlin was number twenty-seven on the Erie Canal. It is made of Medina limestone, smooth except where it was hammered to give better footing. Coping stones are worn at their edges by tow ropes. When open, gates swung into recesses in side walls for ease of passage. These heavy gates could be opened by one man aided by the leverage from a long balance beam which pivoted on a post set in the semi-circular end of the gate recess. The splayed grooves you can see near the post secured metal bracing, and were not tracks for moving parts. A small sluice gate operated by a separate control meant that the large lock gate never had to be pushed against water at a different level.

Past the Canal Park you ride under a railroad tunnel, then up the typically steep north-facing slope of a drumlin. The orchards around you are just a small sample of Wayne County's abundant fruit production; in acres planted, the county leads the state in apples, cherries, and pears. (For a day-long ride through Wayne County orchards see Tour 14.)

23.0 Turn LEFT at the Stop sign onto Lyons-Marengo Road, County Road 344. After crossing the bridge over the Barge Canal and Clyde River, turn LEFT before the railroad tracks, staying on Lyons-Marengo Road.

Keep to the road you are riding, though it changes

name—first becoming Clyde-Marengo Road and then Turn-pike Road. The hamlet of Marengo was once a bustling stagecoach stop on the Montezuma Turnpike, an early privately owned toll road made unprofitable by the Erie Canal.

27.2 Turn RIGHT onto Jenkins Road (unsignposted).

Keep going straight at the Seneca County line, where the name changes to Strang Road, and the signpost may be misleading.

28.0 At the fork, keep LEFT on Strang Road; do not take Bedell Road.

29.3 Continue STRAIGHT at the Stop sign onto Dawson Road.

29.6 Turn RIGHT onto Pucker Road.

30.5 At the Yield sign, turn LEFT onto West Tyre Road.

32.5 At the triangle with an old Sinclair Gasoline sign, turn RIGHT. Ride through the village of Tyre and climb the short hill, keeping the church on your immediate right.

33.8 After crossing over the New York State Thruway, turn LEFT at the first corner, Durling Road.

34.3 Turn RIGHT at the T-junction onto East Tyre Road.

In one-third of a mile you'll arrive at a small parking area giving access to the Esker Brook Nature Trail of the Montezuma National Wildlife Refuge.

35.9 At the Stop sign where you merge with Route 89, bend to the RIGHT, so that you continue south.

36.5 Turn LEFT at the Stop sign onto Routes 5 and 20 East.

38.2 Turn LEFT into the Montezuma National Wildlife Refuge. Your starting point may look the same as when you left, or bird activity hours later may be markedly different.

Nearby bed-and-breakfasts include:
Kreiss Farm, 2097 Highland Fruit Farm Road, Lyons, NY (315-946-9448)

Bicycle shops
Bicycles Today, 88 Grant Avenue, Auburn, NY (315-253-9958)
Geneva Bicycle Center, 493 Exchange Street, Geneva, NY (315-789-5922)
M & R Sports, 286 Clark Street, Auburn, NY (315-252-9069)
Nolan's Sporting Goods, 41 Genesee Street, Auburn, NY (315-252-7249)

16

Bluff Point

27 or 19 miles; mostly easy, with some moderate cycling
Level to slightly undulating, with one long climb
County map: Yates

The prospects over Keuka Lake from many points surrounding its sixty-mile shore line are some of the very finest in the
entire region. Keuka, formerly known as Crooked Lake, is the
only one of the Finger Lakes shaped like a Y; its two north
branches are separated by a high, rounded peninsula, known
as the bluff, fringed with forests and crowned by vineyards.
The road along the peninsula's shore circles back to within a
couple of miles of its starting point; as a result it is used only
by local residents and a few sightseers. About one and a half
miles are unpaved. Following the waterside, tree-shaded,
bluff road, you'll enjoy the longest stretch of quiet lakeside
riding found in any of these tours, and you'll take in exquisite
views of this multi-fingered waterway from elevations accessible with a minimum of hill-climbing. You'll have the oppor-
tunity to fish or swim at beautifully situated Keuka Lake State
Park. A diversion of four miles allows for a second winery visit.
In late September you can attend Penn Yan's Buckwheat
Festival, with various entertainments, cooking demonstrations,
and pancake dinners.

Directions are given from the village of Penn Yan, but those
who want to bicycle less and swim, fish, or wine-taste more,
can cut almost eight miles by driving to Keuka College in
Keuka Park and start the tour there. Fast riders, or those
spending another day in the area, may enjoy simply riding the
seven and a half miles of Skyline Drive along the crest of the
bluff.

Start the tour in front of the post office on Main Street in
Penn Yan, located at the north end of Keuka Lake's east
branch.

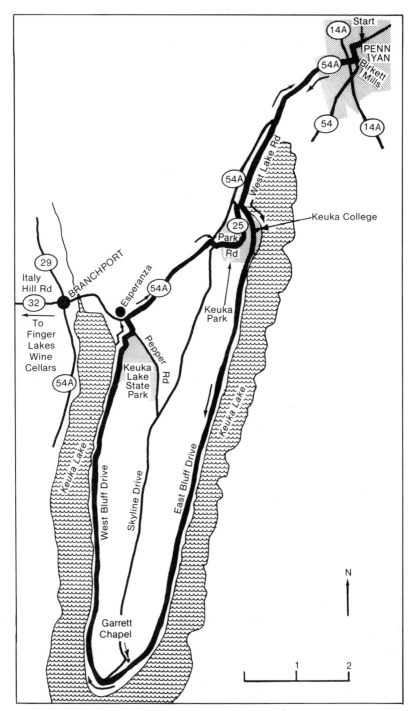

0.0   Ride south on Main Street, toward the business district.

        The town's peculiar name resulted from an 1810 compro-
mise between rival groups of settlers—Pennsylvanians
and New England Yankees. This was some years after the
Wagener family established the first homestead. It was on
their farm that the first Wagener apple was developed,
and Wagener Street, just south of the starting point of this
ride, runs through their former orchard. Birkett Mills, the
largest producer of buckwheat products in the country,
occupies the site of one of Wagener's first grist mills,
where Main Street crosses the Keuka Lake outlet. Visitors
can purchase Birkett products at their modern Main
Street office next to the post office.

        There are many restaurants in and around Penn Yan,
and several grocery stores. There are no other sources for
food on this tour after leaving the village, so you should
carry what you need with you.

0.1   Turn RIGHT at the traffic light onto Elm Street; continue
STRAIGHT across Liberty Street, following the sign for Route
54A.

        In about a mile the Seneca Farms ice cream store on the
left provides covered picnic tables for patrons, plus excellent ice cream. Next to Seneca Farms, Ritchey Road leads
down to Indian Pines Park with swimming and picnicking
facilities.

        At 351 Elm Street, the Wagener Estate Bed and Breakfast
occupies the historic building which was once home to two
of the area's earliest settlers, David and Rebecca Wagener,
in the 1790s. Rates start at $55 for a double (315-536-4591).

1.6   Turn LEFT onto Lower West Lake Road, leaving Route 54A.

        You may have noticed a sign for Jerusalem township. The
name is from the settlement established by followers of
Jemima Wilkinson who came to the wilderness area east
and north of Keuka Lake to set up a "New Jerusalem."
Penn Yan pioneer David Wagener, formerly of Pennsylvania, was one of these "Jemimakins." Wilkinson claimed
that she had died and had come back as the androgy-
nous "Publick Universal Friend," opposed to marriage
and to private property other than her own. Although her
sermons were said to have been almost unintelligible,
"...with sufficient verbosity, with a confused mass of
scriptural quotations, and almost always with obscurity,

which sometimes was impenetrable, " she steadily gath-
ered converts from her native New England and Pennsylvania. As her detractors increased proportionately, she
gave up her original plan of converting the entire world
and sent some of the sect's members in search of a
wilderness retreat in the newly-opened Finger Lakes area.

After they made their initial settlement in the present
town of Milo on the west shore of Seneca Lake in 1788,
dissension among the Jemimakins resulted in the re-
moval of a portion of the group, along with the Friend
herself, to the area now called Jerusalem. There a house
was erected for her in 1815; today it is a private residence
on Friend Hill Road, about six miles west of Penn Yan.

Defections and the obvious limits to the growth of a sect
believing in celibacy reduced the settlement's population; when the Friend "left time" for good in 1819, the sect
disintegrated.

3.7 Turn LEFT at the Stop sign onto Keuka Park Road, County
Road 25.

In about a half mile you'll see the main entrance to the
Keuka College campus on your left. (Begin the tour here if
you want to shorten it by about eight miles.) Ball Hall
(1889), opposite the entrance, dates from the founding of
this four-year women's college; most of the other buildings are modern. The 173-acre campus has over a half
mile of beach front and is the site of the annual mid-
August Keuka Arts Festival. The Dahlstrom Student Center has a cafeteria and bookstore open only during the
academic year, but rest rooms and drinking water are
available throughout the summer.

4.3 Just past the college, keep to the LEFT, onto East Bluff Drive.
Because this road becomes unpaved when it reaches the
tip of the bluff, there is little through traffic. To your left the
east branch of the lake is lined with neat cottages, while
on your right the bluff rises steeply some seven hundred
feet. Chipmunks and woodchucks sun themselves next to
the quiet roadway, and your chances of glimpsing deer
on the wooded bluffside are good.

11.7 At the fork, turn RIGHT onto the unpaved uphill road. (East
Bluff Road Extension becomes unpaved and virtually impas-
sable in a mile or so.)

The uphill climb lasts for six-tenths of a mile and shortly

thereafter you are rewarded with a view of the meeting of the east and west branches of Keuka Lake, and the single trunk extending to the south. The shape resulted from glacial deepening of valleys made by south-flowing streams. The branched lake is now unique in the Finger Lakes. All the Finger Lakes empty to the north, Keuka being again unique in having two inlets, at its northwest and southern tips, with an outlet to the northeast. Thus water entering from the northwest drifts south, rounds the bluff, and flows north to the outlet at Penn Yan.

12.7 Continue STRAIGHT at the intersection with a narrower dirt road.

The exceptional view from Bluff Point has long been appreciated. Charles Williamson, pioneer land agent of the Finger Lakes, chose this as a site for one of his homes; and Abraham Wagener, son of Penn Yan's first settler, built the still surviving Wagener Manor House here in the

Looking north, you see Keuka Lake divide into two branches around Bluff Point.

1830s. More recently it became the site of a chapel built in 1931 by wine magnate Paul Garrett and his wife, in memory of their son, Charles, who died of tuberculosis at the age of twenty-eight. Services are held here at 11:00 a.m. every Sunday in the summer. The chapel is also open Wednesday afternoons from 1:00 to 4:00. To visit the isolated granite memorial and its forested chapel yard, turn right onto the narrow dirt road at the tip of the bluff. You'll reach the chapel after a stiff half-mile climb.

The mile and a half of unpaved road makes a half-circle around the tip of the bluff, and now goes north, becoming West Bluff Drive. The view from the bluff justifies naturalist Samuel Hammond's 1854 proclamation that "there is no more beautiful sheet of water anywhere else in the world than Keuka."

17.9 At the bottom of a long hill, a sign to the right indicates the way to Pepper Road and Skyline Drive. Keep to the LEFT here, passing around a wooden gate (with No Parking and Fire and Ambulance signs) into Keuka Lake State Park.

This 621-acre state park provides facilities for swimming, picnicking, fishing, and boating. There are 150 campsites available mid-May to mid-October. Swimming is excellent in Keuka Lake and many campers bring boats to launch. There are also hiking and bridle trails.

18.9 Part way up a steep climb, turn LEFT to exit the park.

19.2 At the T-junction, turn LEFT onto Pepper Road (unsignposted).

19.7 Turn RIGHT at the Stop sign onto Route 54A.

High on a hill across the road at this junction is an imposing stucco Greek Revival mansion, started in 1823 and completed in 1838. For many years it served as the county poorhouse; in 1979 it became a winery, which operated until 1986.

Those willing to tackle a steep downhill and uphill each way can visit another winery by turning left here instead of right and riding down the hill to the village of Branchport. Continue straight through town and head up Italy Hill Road. In about a mile you'll come to the Finger Lakes Wine Cellars, operated by descendants of Aaron Hunt, who purchased the land in the early nineteenth century. Open Tuesday through Saturday from 10:00 a.m. to 4:00 p.m., this winery offers a half-hour haywagon tour of their vineyards, charging $1.50 for those over ten years of age. The wine shop offers free wine samples. Retrace the two miles to Pepper Road to rejoin the tour.

21.6 Turn RIGHT onto Keuka Park Road (County Road 25), and immediately LEFT at the T-junction.

22.3 Turn LEFT at the Stop sign across from the entrance to Keuka College. (If you elected to begin at the college, the tour ends here.)

22.9 Turn RIGHT onto West Lake Road (County Road 21).

25.0 Turn RIGHT at the Stop sign onto Route 54A.

26.5 Continue STRAIGHT at the traffic light at the intersection of Elm and Liberty.

26.6 Turn LEFT onto Main Street at the traffic light near the post office where the tour began.

A little farther north and on the left at 200 Main Street is the Oliver House. Built in 1852 and used as a home by three generations of doctors, it now houses the Yates County Historical Society. Some personal belongings of Jemima Wilkinson are preserved here plus other items of local history. The house is open from 9:00 a.m. to 5:00 p.m. Monday through Friday.

Nearby bed and breakfasts include:
Finton's Landing, 661 E. Lake Road, Penn Yan, NY (315-536-3146)
Four Seasons B&B, 470 W. Lake Road, Branchport, NY (607-868-4686)
The Fox Inn, 158 Main Street, Penn Yan, NY (315-536-3101)
Heirlooms B&B, 2756 Coates Road, Penn Yan, NY (315-536-7682)
Keuka Lake Gone With the Wind, 453 W. Lake Road, Branchport, NY (607-868-4603)
On the Beach, 191 W. Lake Road, Penn Yan, NY (315-536-4646)
Wagener Estate B&B, 351 Elm Street, Penn Yan, NY (315-536-4591)

Bicycle shops
Geneva Bicycle Center, 493 Exchange Street, Geneva, NY (315-789-5922)
Weaver Bicycle Shop, 1220 Route 14A, Penn Yan, NY (315-536-3012)

17

Watkins Glen—Hector Wineries

21 miles; easy to moderate cycling
Gradual ascents and descents, undulating hills, some level land
County Map: Schuyler

World-famous Watkins Glen State Park attracts thousands of visitors every year, as does the Grand Prix Race Track, so traffic in the little village of Watkins Glen can be heavy during the summer season. Starting at the park entrance in the center of town, this route leads you out of the business district quickly and easily, to head north along a road that is not usually heavily traveled, despite its state route designation and lake view. Along this highway you'll have a chance to tour two small farm wineries, with the option of visiting three more. All allow you to sample their products. You'll also go by the only section of national forest land in New York State, with opportunities for wilderness camping, hiking and picnicking. About half-way through the ride is a two-and-a-half-mile stretch of well-graded, unpaved road.

Much of the appeal of this route lies in the ease with which it carries you to scenic heights overlooking Seneca Lake and gently tilts you back down to water level again. A walk through the labyrinthine gorge at Watkins Glen State Park, with its cascades, grottoes and dizzying heights, provides a splendid complement to your ride. You might cap your walk with a dip in the park's Olympic-size pool—a perfect ending to a perfect day.

0.0 From the main entrance of Watkins Glen State Park, cross Franklin Street and ride east on unsignposted Tenth Street, the street between the Tourist Information Center and the county offices.

In addition to its famous state park, Watkins Glen is known for its three-million-dollar Grand Prix Race Track.

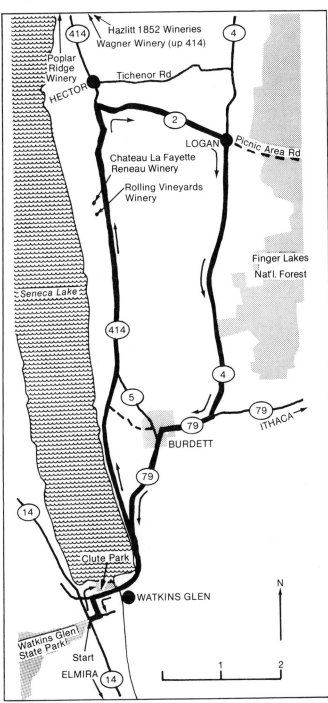

Hazlitt 1852 Wineries
Wagner Winery (up 414)

Poplar
Ridge
Winery

HECTOR

Tichenor Rd

LOGAN

Picnic Area Rd

Chateau La Fayette
Reneau Winery

Rolling Vineyards
Winery

Finger Lakes

Nat'l. Forest

~Seneca Lake~

ITHACA

BURDETT

Clute Park

WATKINS GLEN

N

Watkins Glen
State Park

Start

ELMIRA

In the village, at 110 North Franklin Street, the National Motor Racing Museum is open daily in July and August from 10:00 a.m. to 4:00 p.m., and the same hours on weekends in June and September. Admission is $1.00 for adults and $.50 for children.

There are a few restaurants and food stores in Watkins Glen. Apart from a small restaurant near the tour's beginning, there are no other sources of food along this route.

0.1   Turn LEFT at the first intersection onto North Decatur Street. You may notice that the numbered streets in the village are indicated by small race cars with numbers on the sides.

0.4   At the traffic light, turn RIGHT onto Fourth Street, Route 414 North.

Soon you'll cross the Seneca Lake inlet which was enlarged in 1830 as a spur of the Chemung Canal. The canal connected Seneca Lake with cities to the south. This spur extends just three miles to Montour Falls, and is the only portion of the Chemung still maintained.

You'll also pass the Watkins Salt Company on the left, now a subsidiary of Cargill. This plant and that of the International Salt Company two miles up the west side of the lake, have been pumping brine for nearly a hundred years from the vast salt deposits underlying the area. International's plant, which you'll see across the lake, looks somewhat like a power plant because heat is used to evaporate water from the brine. Sites connected with the salt industry are passed on Captain Bill's narrated Seneca Lake Cruise, which leaves from the foot of Franklin Street. It operates May 15th through October 15th seven days a week and charges $5.75 for adults and $2.75 for children. The schedule is obtained by calling 607-535-4541.

1.9   Part way up the hill, take the LEFT fork, staying on Route 414 North.

The climb up from Watkins Glen is gradual and affords time to inspect the exposed shale beds, a common formation in the southern Finger Lakes. Most waterfalls in the area are maintained by erosion-resistant sandstone overlaying beds of weak shale.

In a little over a mile and a half you'll pass Hector Falls, known earlier as Factory Falls because of the mills, foundry, and potash works clustered here. Hector Falls illustrates a common feature of the Finger Lakes region, the hanging valley. Waterfalls resulted when glaciers down-cut deeply in north-south streambeds (Seneca Lake, for example, reaches a depth of 632 feet), leaving east-west tributaries well above the new valley floors. Next to these falls is the Chalet Leon Motel, a health resort and tea room.

Four miles farther is the Rolling Vineyards Winery, opened in 1981. This is one of the small wineries which have recently been springing up at the rate of a few a year in response to a 1975 state law known as the Farm Wineries Act. Spending only $125 for a farm winery license and $25 more for wholesale and retail licenses, any grape owner can produce and sell up to 50,000 gallons of wine yearly. The intent of the bill—to give growers an alternative to selling their grapes at low prices to the few big wineries—seems to be succeeding. The public also benefits by getting a greater variety and higher quality of wines.

Rolling Vineyards grows eighteen varieties of grapes on native, hybrid, and European vines. The winery is open for short tours and tastings Monday through Saturday from 10:00 a.m. to 5:00 p.m., and Sunday noon to 5:00, May through October.

Just over a mile beyond the winery a sign indicates the road to lakeside Smith Park, where picnic tables are provided in secluded woodland groves and there are opportunities for camping and swimming.

9.0 Turn RIGHT onto County Road 2.

A half-mile farther north on 414 is the village of Hector. Hector was part of the Military Tract, that portion of Western New York set aside for Revolutionary War veterans. The tract was divided into twenty-five townships of sixty thousand acres each, with each township receiving a classical name.

Those interested in visiting more wineries can continue north on Route 414. Two-and-one-half miles past the junction with County Road 2 is Hazlitt 1852 Vineyards, just north of Hazlitt is Poplar Ridge Winery at Valois, and about three miles beyond that is Wagner Winery.

11.3 Turn RIGHT at the Stop sign onto County Road 4.

A sign at the corner of Picnic Area Road in the hamlet of Logan points up the hill to the main recreation site of Finger Lakes National Forest, the only national forest land in New York. Although settlers tried to farm the Hector Hills throughout the 1800s, poor soil caused most of the farms to be abandoned by 1900. In 1934 the Federal government began acquiring land, reforesting hundreds of acres, adding twenty-five ponds for wildlife, and establishing common pasturage. Today the Hector Cooperative Grazing Association grazes about 2,100 head of cattle from May to October.

The area's recreational facilities include the Blueberry Patch Campground with nine sites, and twenty-five miles of hiking trails. There is a fee for camping at Blueberry Patch, but camping in undeveloped areas is free. A map and further information are available from District Ranger, U.S. Forest Service, 208 Broadway, P.O. Box W, Montour Falls, NY 14865 (607-535-7369).

Ideally, mid-nineteenth-century octagon houses were supposed to have a raised main floor, an encircling porch, and a low-pitched roof.

As you ride along County Road 4, to your left you'll see the formation called the Hector Backbone rising to a height of 1,880 feet. From here the route descends gradually all the way to Watkins Glen.

16.0   Where County Road 4 ends, turn RIGHT at the Stop sign onto Route 79 (unsignposted).

16.8   Pass through the village of Burdett, turning LEFT to continue on Route 79.

Watkins Glen's thirty-five-acre Clute Park at the southeast tip of the lake has facilities for picnicking and swimming, plus a small food concession. Campsites are available opposite the park.

20.3   In Watkins Glen, turn LEFT at the traffic light onto Decatur Street.

20.6   Turn RIGHT onto Tenth Street, which ends at the State Park entrance where the tour began.

In 1863 newspaperman Morvalden Ells saw commercial potential in the wet and winding glen beside the village of Watkins. Constructing a tortuous path along, above, and behind the numerous waterfalls and cascades, Ells opened what he called "Freer's Glen" on July 4th of that Civil War year and laid the foundation for one of the best-known state parks in the world. The site was further developed by the State Parks Commission in 1924. A free guide to the one-and-a-half-mile gorge trail is available at the park entrance, and nightly, Timespell, the much acclaimed sound and laser light show, takes place here. The park has 305 campsites and a 50-meter pool, both reached from Route 419.

Neighboring Montour Falls has further examples of gorge geology with twenty waterfalls within a mile radius of the business district. Chequaga Falls tumbles from 156 feet above the west end of Main Street. In the Louvre in Paris hangs a 1795 sketch of the cataract done by King Louis Philippe when he stayed at the Old Brick Tavern, now a museum at 108 North Catharine Street.

Wine enthusiasts may want to visit some of the wineries on the west side of Seneca Lake. In the twenty-five miles between Watkins Glen and the village of Dresden are five of the region's better-known farm wineries. Because they are along busy Route 14 we don't suggest that they be visited by bicycle. With a car, however, one could spend a pleasant afternoon visiting (south to north): Giasi Winery, in Rock

Stream; Glenora Wine Cellars, in Glenora; Hermann J. Wiemer Vineyard, near Dundee; Four Chimneys Farm Winery, in Himrod; and Prejean Winery, near Dresden.

Nearby-bed-and-breakfasts include:
Catharine Creek B&B, RD#1 Box 109, Montour Falls, NY (607-535-4113)
Country Gardens, P.O. Box 67, Burdett, NY (607-546-2272)
Peach Orchard B&B, Peach Orchard Road, Hector, NY (607-546-2593)
Red House Country Inn, Picnic Area Road, Burdett, NY (607-546-8566)
Victorian B&B, 216 North Madison Avenue, Watkins Glen, NY (607-535-6582)
Vintage View, Box 245, Watkins Glen, NY (607-535-7909)

Bicycle shops
Corning Bike Works, 96 East Market Street, Corning, NY (607-962-7831)
Hillside Bicycles, 75 Bridge Street, Corning, NY (607-936-8124)
Kingsbury's Cyclery, 204 South Main Street, Elmira, NY (607-733-3465)
Little's Bicycles, 1074 South Main Street, Elmira, NY (607-733-3833)
Pedaler's Choice Bikes, 13th and College Avenue, Elmira Heights, NY (607-733-4813)
Qumar, 220 Roe Avenue, Elmira, NY (607-732-0278)

18

Hammondsport Wineries

3 to 14 miles; easy cycling
Mostly level, with hilly optional rides
County map: Steuben

Hammondsport is the hub of the major wine-producing region of the eastern United States. The area produces a greater variety of table wines than any other in the world. The industry was a thriving one in the second half of the nineteenth century, but only four companies here survived Prohibition. Today there are five wineries in the area bordering Keuka Lake, and over thirty-five in the Finger Lakes region with new small wineries appearing each year. Informative brochures are available from the New York Wine-Grape Foundation, Elm and Liberty Street, Penn Yan, NY 14527.

Although five other tours in this book include winery visits, wineries are this tour's *raison d'etre*. The tour uses Pulteney Square, the village green in Hammondsport, as base for short rides, to nearby wineries, out-and-back rides, rather than a circular tour. Designed to visit as many wineries in as few miles as possible, the route offers short and easy excursions, allowing time for tours of each winery and for recuperation between wine-tasting sessions.

In the Dublin-based *Irish Times*, reports of arrests for cycling while intoxicated are not uncommon. Arrests for such violations are more rare in the United States; nonetheless, cycling while impaired can be hazardous—to cyclists as well as to others. Ample time should be allowed for the effects of a generous wine-tasting to dissipate, particularly on summer days when hot air and blazing sun contrast stunningly with a cool wine cellar. And no one will take offense if you decline any, or all, of the free samples offered.

The rides start at the square in the village of Hammondsport at the south end of Keuka Lake. The following directions lead to the De May cellars, and to Taylor, Great Western, and Gold Seal.

0.0 From Pulteney Square ride uphill on Sheather Street, passing
to the left of the First Presbyterian Church (1847).

Hammondsport earned its name as a port during the
1830s when construction of the seven-mile Crooked Lake
Canal from the northern tip of Keuka Lake to the west side
of Seneca Lake linked it with the Erie Canal. Canal boats
loaded with grain, lumber and farm products were towed
by steamer over the lake and thence to the canal system.
By the 1850s, the construction of the Erie Railroad to the
south of Hammondsport severely reduced the town's
importance as a port, and by 1870 the Crooked Lake
Canal was abandoned altogether.

In 1872, Hammondsport's first bonded winery, the

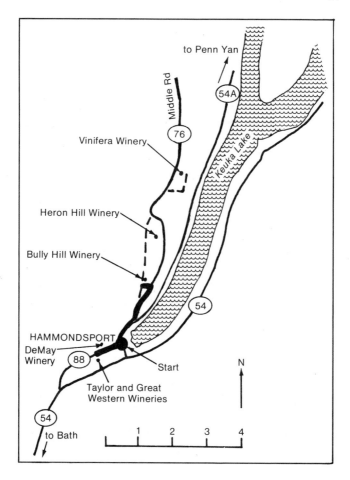

Pleasant Valley Company, built the eight-mile-long, single-track Bath and Hammondsport Railroad to link the wine village with the railroad. Known as the Champagne Trail, the little line's slogan was "Not as long as the others, but just as wide." The line still ships wine and grapes; its office is in the 1877 train depot next to the village's lakeside park. Kids swim here unofficially; sanctioned bathing is at Champlin Beach a mile from town at the junction of Routes 54 and 54A.

There are several restaurants and a grocery store bordering the square, plus other restaurants around Keuka Lake.

0.1 Turn LEFT at the Stop sign onto Main Street, and at the next intersection turn RIGHT onto Lake Street (County Road 88).

Wild grapes, small and often bitter, grew in the Finger Lakes for millennia before the arrival of man, but the first cultivated varieties were brought to Hammondsport in 1829 by William Bostwick, minister of St. James Episcopal Church, on a corner of Main and Lake Streets. Behind his rectory, Bostwick planted Catawba and Isabella vines from the Hudson Valley. Commercial wine production did not begin until 1860, when French winemaker C. D. Champlin founded the Pleasant Valley Wine Company and was granted U. S. Winery License No.1. The Pleasant Valley Wine Company and its Great Western Label became part of the Taylor Wine Company in 1962, and Taylor in turn was acquired by the Coca-Cola Company in 1977, which along with Gold Seal, subsequently became part of Seagrams.

On another corner of Lake and Main Streets is the library and Glenn H. Curtiss Museum. Glenn Hammond Curtiss was born among the glens of Hammondsport in 1878. As had the Wright brothers, Curtiss began his aviation career by operating a bicycle shop—his faced the square in his native village. Soon Curtiss had a bike with a motor added; by 1907 he had set a land speed record of 136.7 miles per hour in an eight-cylinder motorcycle of his own design. At the same time, Curtiss, in association with Alexander Graham Bell and others, were experimenting with flight—often at Hammondsport. A long series of Curtiss firsts and prizes followed: first pre-announced and witnessed flight of one kilometer in

America, first pilot's license, New York *World* prize of
$10,000 for flying from Albany to New York City, operator
of the first pilot-training school, first successful landing
and takeoff from a ship—signalling the start of naval
aviation. Curtiss Company planes fought in the First World
War, and thousands of pilots trained in the famous Curtiss
"Jenny." Machines from little Hammondsport carried the
name of a local boy a long way.

The museum contains many of the actual planes, hydro-
planes, motorcycles, and other devices which Curtiss
created, plus displays reflecting his times. These occupy
several floors in what was once a school, built in 1852.
Open hours are 9:00 a.m. to 5:00 p.m. Monday through
Saturday from May 1st to October 31st, plus Sunday in
July, August and September. Admission is $2.00 for adults,
$1.00 for teenagers and senior citizens, and $.50 for young-
sters from seven to twelve. Mercury Aircraft, which you'll
pass on the left as you ride down Lake Street, is an offshoot
of the original Curtiss Company. The village and wine

Most Finger Lakes wineries welcome visitors for tours and tastings.
Pictured is the DeMay winery at Hammondsport.

country information kiosk is behind the museum.

Many of the fine homes along Lake Street were built by winery owners and winemakers during the second half of the nineteenth century. About a mile from the village is the small De May Wine Cellars. De May is a family operation begun in 1977 by natives of the Loire Valley of France. Visitors may be surprised to have the virtues of American wines extolled by enthusiastic salespeople with Maurice Chevalier accents. Champagne fermented in the bottle in the traditional manner accounts for about seventy percent of the winery's 10,000 gallon yearly production. Free tastings are given 10:00 a.m. to 5:00 p.m. Monday through Saturday, and on Sunday afternoon in September and October.

1.6 Turn LEFT, following signs to the visitor's parking for the Taylor and Pleasant Valley Wineries.

The combined Taylor/Great Western/Gold Seal tour is the most elaborate among wineries, as might be expected from the largest producers. Walking distances are shortened by bus rides to and from the Visitor Center. At Taylor stainless steel and modern equipment predominate, though oak barrels are used for the aging of fine sherries. Tastings are conducted at tables in a former wine cellar; generous amounts of five wines are sampled. It is also possible to taste wines at the Visitor Center either after, or instead of, taking the tour. At the Visitor Center shop, wine, accessories, T-shirts, and more are for sale. On the spacious grounds is Taylor Park, with picnic tables, charcoal grills, and a trout stream. The Visitor Center is open 10:00 a.m. to 4:00 p.m. Monday through Saturday, noon to 4:00 p.m. on Sunday, July through October, and 11:00 a.m. to 3:00 p.m. Monday through Saturday the rest of the year. Tours are offered Monday through Friday *only.*

3.2 Retracing your route out brings you back to Hammondsport.

The other major winery route takes you to Bully Hill (el. 1,375) with possibilities of side trips to another winery or two. This route is very hilly, and is not for wine-weakened legs.

0.0 From the northeast corner of the square (near the Hammondsport Ambulance Corps building) take the LEFT fork, following the sign to 54A.

0.2   At the fork, go LEFT, uphill, on County Road 76, Middle Road.

1.6   To get to Bully Hill Winery, turn LEFT up the steep, partially paved road.

As is frequently the case in Europe, many Finger Lakes vineyards are on steep hillsides, often above bodies of water. The slopes provide good drainage, preventing a too-watery grape and saving the roots from rotting. Long and deep lakes give up their heat slowly, easing the danger of early frosts. Conversely, after the freezing winter, the lakes keep their surroundings cool, preventing premature budding which could expose the blooms to a late frost. Grapes need at least 120 days between killing frosts; they can usually count on 135 in the Finger Lakes. Picking is concentrated from the second week of September through October, the most interesting time to visit the wineries—and the busiest.

Bully Hill is run by Walter S. Taylor. Free Bully Hill tours, offered 10:00 a.m. to 4:30 p.m. Monday through Saturday, and 1:00 p.m. to 4:30 p.m. on Sunday, May 1st to October 31st, include a tour of the vineyards, weather permitting. Also on the premises is the Greyton H. Taylor Wine Museum, with art work by "Mr. No Name, Owner of the Estate," a Winemakers Gift Shop, and the Champagne Country Cafe, serving from 11:30 a.m. to 4:30 p.m. Bed and breakfast accommodations are offered in two homes on the estate, one of which is the 1885 house of George and Walter Taylor, founders of the original Taylor Wine Company.

4.4   Retracing your outward route brings you back to Hammondsport.

While riding toward Bully Hill, you may have noticed signs for Heron Hill or Vinifera Wineries. Both grow only vinifera grapes, although Heron Hill buys non-vinifera from other growers. And both sell estate-bottled wine on the premises.

Heron Hill's Johannesberg Riesling has won eight consecutive gold medals in national competition. The winery enjoys a magnificent view over Keuka Lake from its location above Middle Road (County Road 76), about two miles past the Bully Hill turnoff. Heron Hill has a bright, attractive tasting room; tables are available inside and on the flower-bedecked terrace. The tasting room is open weekdays 10:00 a.m. to 5:00 p.m. and 1:00 to 5:00 p.m. on Sunday,

May through November; phone 607-868-4241.

Originally from the Ukraine, the late Konstantin Frank was the pioneer in the growing *Vitis vinifera* (European) grapes in the Finger Lakes. *Vitis labrusca* (native) vines (Concord, Catawba, Niagara, Delaware, Dutchess, and more) can stand temperatures well below zero and are excellent for juice, jam, and jelly. Dr. Frank proved that vinifera grapes, particularly Chardonnay and Riesling, could survive New York winters. Getting to Vinifera requires a right turn onto unpaved Wright Road, one-and-a-half miles past (north of) Heron Hill. After a mile of steep and unpaved road, you'll reach the winery. This last is recommended only for rough-riding enthusiasts. Visitors should phone for an appointment; Vinifera's number is 607-868-4884.

Even if you've had enough of wineries, we recommend a couple of miles of riding on Middle Road north of the turnoff for Bully Hill. The view of Keuka Lake and Bluff Point, where Keuka splits to the north, may be the finest in the Finger Lakes.

Nearby bed-and-breakfasts include:
Another Tyme, 7 Church Street, Box 134, Hammondsport, NY (607-569-2747)
Blushing Rose B&B Inn, 11 William Street, Hammondsport, NY (607-569-3402)
Bowman House, 61 Lake Street, Box 586, Hammondsport, NY (607-569-2516)
Cedar Beach B&B, 642 West Lake Road, RD #2 Box 137, Hammondsport, NY (607-868-3228)
Lake Keuka Manor, 626 West Lake Road, Hammondsport, NY (607-868-3276)
Park Inn Hotel, Village Square, Hammondsport, NY (607-569-9387)
Pleasant Valley B&B, Lake Street Extension, RD #3 Box 69, Hammondsport, NY (607-569-3472)
Willows B&B, 7615 South Valley Road, Hammondsport, NY (607-569-2447)

Bicycle shops
Corning Bike Works, 96 East Market Street, Corning, NY (607-962-7831)
Hillside Bicycles, 75 Bridge Street, Corning, NY (607-936-8124)
Snyder's Wheels Unlimited, 20 West Steuben Street, Bath, NY (607-776-6609)
Weaver Bicycle Shop, 1220 Route 14A, Penn Yan, NY (315-536-3012)

19

Steuben County Valleys

28 or 36 miles; moderate cycling
Gentle climbs with one steep section and some level terrain
County map: Steuben

Hidden in the southwest corner of the Finger Lakes, the valleys visited on this tour are sparsely settled. Even on a holiday weekend you can ride here through miles of sylvan quiet. About half of the tour is spent on the Whitman-Spalding Highway, a road with a wide paved shoulder and a surface so smooth that even riding uphill seems effortless. Most of the rest of the tour follows an almost traffic-free country road through the forested valley of Tenmile Creek. As there is little need to look at a map or read directions (you simply ride one road up to Prattsburg and another back), the pure pleasure of rural cycling can be enjoyed to the full.

Great things were expected of Bath, the major village here, and the starting point for this tour. Land agent extraordinaire Charles Williamson, representing the English Pulteney syndicate, laid out Bath's Pulteney Square in 1793, believing he was designing the capital of the frontier. At the head of the Cohocton River, Bath seemed sure to become a major shipping center for trade down the Susquehanna River to Baltimore. But the completion of the Erie Canal in 1825 shifted trade routes to the north and east, and population and economic growth went that way, too. Cyclists enjoying this uncrowded region will be grateful for Williamson's miscalculation.

The tour begins at Pulteney Square in the Steuben County village of Bath. (The route can be shortened by some eight miles by starting instead at Kanona, northwest of Bath.)

0.0   From the square in Bath, ride west on West Steuben Street. Bath was honored with the name of the Pulteney family's ancestral home in England. On its grand square Williamson established his land office and nearby built a race track and theater. In handbills distributed to gentlefolk from Boston to Richmond, Williamson promised "trusty guides to meet and conduct gentlemen and their suites to the far-famed city on the upper reaches of the Susquehanna, in the land of crystal lakes and memorial parks, located in the garden home of the lately vanquished Iroquois." Clever promotion brought Bath's population to 800 within three years. Williamson built a mansion for himself on nearby Lake Salubria, but he was destined never to live there. Williamson was estranged from his wife and he lost his young daughter to Genesee Fever (malaria); by 1801 his extravagance in spending a million dollars on his Finger Lakes wilderness got him recalled to

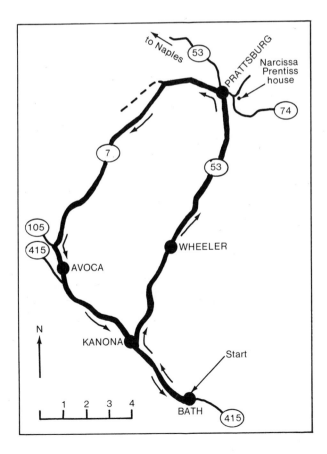

England. Five years later he died of yellow fever on a West Indies-bound ship.

Bath's brief boom as a shipping center ended two decades later. Williamson's land office was pulled down in this century, and little remains of his legacy save the square he designed and his little daughter's grave in the pioneer cemetery on West Steuben Street.

There are groceries and restaurants in Bath, and at the tour's half-way point, Prattsburg has a small grocery and a snack shop.

0.8   Pass the Ramada Inn and continue STRAIGHT at the traffic light, following Route 415 North.

3.7   Turn RIGHT at Kanona onto Route 53. Continue through Kanona, turning RIGHT to stay on Route 53.

Formerly Kennedyville, Kanona, or "rusty water" to the Indians, once constructed coastal vessels which were floated downriver and sold in Baltimore.

Within a mile or so a sign proclaims that this road is called the Whitman-Spalding Highway, honoring two local men who became pioneer missionaries in the American west. The odd twist in the story is that Marcus Whitman was a doctor who wanted to be a minister, and Henry Spalding was a minister who wanted the woman Whitman married. Nonetheless, Whitman and his wife, Narcissa Prentiss, and Spalding and his second-choice spouse, Eliza, set out together to the Oregon Territory in 1836, the women becoming the first whites of their sex to cross the Rockies.

About four miles from Kanona is the hamlet of Wheeler, where Dr. Whitman worked for several years as a young physician. Here the Wheeler Bed and Breakfast, on the right, provides accommodations in an 1867 Greek Revival home.

15.1   At the far end of the square in Prattsburg, turn LEFT onto Chapel Street, County Road 7.

Prattsburg has a grocery store and a snack shop, with drinking water available on the village green.

Narcissa Prentiss and Henry Spalding attended the Franklin Academy in Prattsburg. The house in which she was born and spent her early years is open to the public Wednesday through Sunday 1:00 to 5:00 p.m. from about the end of June to about Labor Day. No admission is charged. To see it, turn right (east) at the green onto

Mechanic Street. In one-half mile take the second left fork (County Road 75, not Mill Street); the house is the first one on the right.

The Prentiss house was probably the first frame dwelling in the area. There Narcissa seems to have absorbed a sense of religious purpose from parents said never to laugh for fear of appearing frivolous. Her missionary zeal was formed independent of Dr. Whitman. She asked the Presbyterian Missionary Board if unmarried females were wanted; at about that time Whitman was planning a long westward expedition and settlement. Each could well use a spouse-companion. Their honeymoon trip included the Spaldings and assorted fur company traders; it lasted 2,250 miles and involved hauling the first wagon over what was to be called the Oregon Trail.

In 1847, near Walla Walla, Washington, Dr. Whitman, his wife and twelve other whites were killed by Cayuse Indians—directly, because they were blamed for a deadly

Small pioneer cemeteries recall the settlement of the Finger Lakes region, now almost two hundred years ago.

measles epidemic; perhaps indirectly, because of rage that the Indian way of life was being erased from America. Henry Spalding had spent the previous night at the Whitmans' house and escaped by only hours. He lived to be an old man and died in Idaho.

When you leave Prattsburg, the rather tough uphill lasts for a mile and a half, climbing to over 2,100 feet. But once the climb is over you have a wonderful, miles-long downhill.

17.2 Follow the paved road to the LEFT; don't take the dirt road.

The valley of Tenmile Creek has only a few small farmsteads. The largely hardwood forest is bright orange-red in autumn.

26.5 Turn LEFT at the Stop sign onto County Road 105. In the village of Avoca, cross the railroad tracks and continue straight through town.

Once called Podunk, Avoca's name was changed to grant the dying wish of a resident.

28.5 At the Stop sign, turn LEFT onto Route 415 South.

32.3 If you started at Kanona, turn LEFT here into the village, If not, continue on Route 415 toward Bath.

35.2 At the traffic light, take the RIGHT fork, so that the Steuben Inn is to your left. Retracing your outward route will bring you to the square in Bath in less than a mile.

Bath's modern Steuben Inn has a swimming pool and a restaurant.

To learn more about Bath you can visit the village museum, Elm Cottage, at 28 Cameron Street, south of the river. In July and August it is open Monday through Friday 9:00 a.m. to 4:00 p.m., and Sunday afternoon 1:00 to 4:00. On the way you'll pass the town library, established in a fine 1829 building which was once the home of railroad magnate John Magee.

Nearby bed and breakfasts include:
Wheeler B&B, RD#2, Box 455, Bath, NY (607-776-6756)

Bicycle shops
Corning Bike Works, 96 East Market Street, Corning, NY (607-962-7831)
Hillside Bicycles, 75 Bridge Street, Corning, NY (607-939-8124)
Snyder's Wheels Unlimited, 20 West Steuben Street, Bath, NY (607-776-6609)

20

Corning—Harris Hill

32 miles; easy cycling
Flat terrain, with one big hill
County maps: Chemung, Steuben

All of this tour is in the wide, flat valley of the Chemung River except (there's always a catch, isn't there?) for one big hill. Harris Hill rises steeply 700 feet from the valley floor. On its breezy top you'd expect to find kids flying kites or tossing model airplanes into the wind—and in a way that's true. This hill is known as the Glider Capital of America, the traditional center for sailplane enthusiasts. A sleek, modern building houses the National Soaring Museum, where the latest display techniques and audio-visual devices explain the history and mystery of soaring. Sailplanes take off and land in front of the museum; if you go for a ride in a two-seater, it will surely be the high point of your trip. More mundane pleasures in Harris Hill Park include an excellent swimming pool.

The tour begins in the City of Corning, with its famous Corning Glass Works, home of Steuben Glass. The Museum of Glass deserves all the superlatives it has received. Simply, it shouldn't be missed. And downtown Corning is a very pleasant surprise, having benefitted from one of the most innovative and successful renewal efforts of recent years. Anyone remembering Corning before the 1972 flood will be amazed.

The tour starts at Baron Steuben Place, at the center of Corning's Market Street restoration district.

0.0 From Baron Steuben Place, ride east on Market Street.
Perhaps what is best about refurbished Market Street is that it is authentic. It does not try to import a Colonial past which Corning never had, or line its streets with trendy boutiques. The late-Victorian brick and terra cotta facades have been exposed, cleaned, repaired. Overall

planning and design advice was and is provided by the Market Street Restoration Agency, which also saw to the planting of trees and the installation of the brick sidewalk; but improvements to individual buildings are made by the owners.

At Baron Steuben Place, the Wine Center provides a convenient introduction to the products of about twenty Finger Lakes farm wineries. The tasting room is open

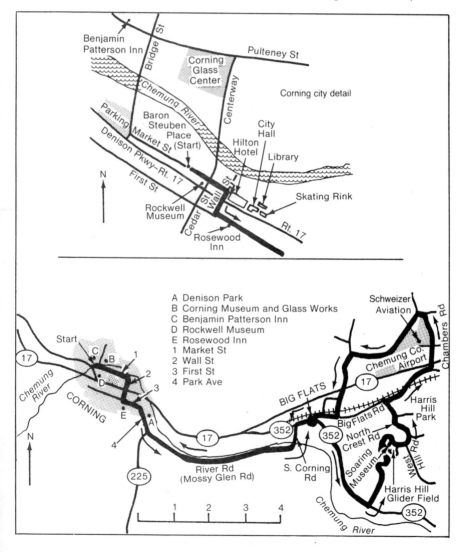

A Denison Park
B Corning Museum and Glass Works
C Benjamin Patterson Inn
D Rockwell Museum
E Rosewood Inn
1 Market St
2 Wall St
3 First St
4 Park Ave

Monday through Saturday 11:00 a.m. to 8:00 p.m. The Center also has a sales room and a fascinating exhibit area highlighting the history and lore of wine and current wine-making practice.

0.3 When Market Street ends, turn RIGHT. Cross Denison Parkway (Route 17), and turn LEFT at the next corner, onto First Street.

The modern buildings at the end of Market Street are limited in height to harmonize with the old shops. The Hilton Inn is followed by the Glass Workers Union building and City Hall. Across the plaza is a beautiful public library; unifying the space is a covered outdoor ice rink, where you may find kids playing lacrosse in summer. A December 1976 article in *Architectural Record* has more on the design details.

Corning has many restaurants and food stores, and there is a concession stand at Harris Hill Park, at the tour's halfway point.

1.1 By the triangle with the Civil War obelisk, turn RIGHT onto Park Avenue, Route 225.

2.2 Where Route 225 turns right, continue STRAIGHT on Park Avenue, which becomes River Street (also called Mossy Glen Road) outside the city limits.

7.2 After crossing over the Chemung River, turn RIGHT at the Stop sign onto Route 352 East.

Near Big Flats the wide valley floor divides around Harris Hill. It is believed that the Chemung River once flowed north of the hill, having cut the more direct southerly course toward Elmira post-glacially, in perhaps the last 10,000 years. The bike route follows the new river gorge between steep-sided ridges.

11.0 Turn LEFT onto Harris Hill Road, also following a sign to the National Soaring Museum.

The uphill lasts for about a mile and a half, and is the only climb on the route. At the top, where there is a spectacular view over the valley, a turn to the right leads to the Soaring Museum and the glider field. The museum is open daily 10:00 a.m. to 5:00 p.m.

What most of us call gliders are more accurately called sailplanes, and purists prefer "soaring" to "gliding" to describe their sport. Old-fashioned gliders could only descend; they lost altitude slowly, but they were always on the way down. In truly bird-like style, modern sailplanes can gain altitude, soaring up on ridge or thermal lifts, like hawks.

If you go for a sailplane ride (which costs $25) you'll sit in the front seat, with an unobstructed view. At about 3,000 feet your tow plane dives to the left, the tow rope is released, and you soar up to the right. The motor hum fades; you hear the wind. Harris Hill, forested ridges, valley farms, highways, and ponds are below. You may find a thermal, a bubble of rising warm air, and circle upward. Sailplane rides at Harris Hill are given by soaring club members on weekends throughout the year, and daily in summer. Rides are given daily at the Schweizer Soaring School at Chemung County Airport, which is passed later on this route.

From the glider field, return to the main road and continue over the crest of the hill. You'll descend through lovely Harris Hill Park, with excellent picnic facilities, a snack shop, rest rooms, and a big swimming pool ($1 admission).

13.4 With the swimming pool to your right, take the LEFT fork, so that after the turn the golf driving range is to your right.

13.8 Turn LEFT at the Stop sign onto West Hill Road; also following an Airport sign.

14.0 At the Stop sign, turn LEFT onto North Crest Road.

15.2 Turn RIGHT at the Stop sign, again following a sign to the airport.

16.9 Turn LEFT onto Chambers Road.

In less than a mile after crossing over the highway and passing a shopping center you'll see a sign to the left to Schweizer Aviation. Schweizer, the leading maker of sailplanes, also operates a major soaring school. Appointments for sailplane rides are recommended, but you often have a good chance of getting aboard just by showing up and waiting. As mentioned earlier, rides are given every day, weather permitting. In general, morning rides are smoother, while real upward soaring is more likely in the afternoon. For an extra fee you can get an introductory soaring lesson and try your hands at the controls—while knowing the pilot behind you has no intention of letting you end his flying career. Schweizer's phone number is 607-739-3821.

18.6 Turn LEFT at the Stop sign, still following signs to the airport.

18.9 Once again, turn LEFT at the Stop sign.

21.5 Turn LEFT at the Stop sign; and in about a mile, continue STRAIGHT at the traffic light, crossing Route 17.

22.9 As the road curves right, take the LEFT fork onto Winters Road, passing under a low railroad bridge.

23.3 Turn RIGHT at the Stop sign onto Big Flats Road (unsign-posted).

24.1 At the Yield sign, turn RIGHT onto Route 352 West (unsign-posted).

24.6 Turn LEFT onto South Corning Road.

30.7 At the Civil War monument, turn LEFT onto East First Street.

> To your right at this corner is Denison Park, which has a pond, picnic tables, grills, rest rooms, and a swimming pool. The pool is on the far side of a tunnel; it's open daily 1:00 to 8:00 p.m.

32.2 After passing the hospital, turn RIGHT onto Wall Street. Go STRAIGHT across Denison Parkway; turning LEFT at the next corner will bring you to Market Street, near where the tour began.

> Corning has more of interest than can be packed into a day of cycling. The Museum of Glass has one of the finest

Harris Hill is home to the National Soaring Museum. Sailplane rides are given at Harris Hill and at nearby Schweizer Aviation.

collections in the world in an imaginative new (1980) building designed by Gunnar Birkerts. Exhibits illustrate 3,500 years of glass making. One admission of $2.50 covers entry to all four sections of the Glass Center, which is open daily 9:00 a.m. to 5:00 p.m.

The Benjamin Patterson Inn, 59 West Pulteney Street, was built in 1796 by the seemingly ubiquitous Charles Williamson. The historical society operates the inn as a museum, charging $1.00 admission; hours are weekdays 10:00 a.m. to noon and 1:00 to 4:00 p.m. The Rockwell Museum, at Denison Parkway and Cedar Street, has the largest collection of Western art in the east; works by Frederic Remington, Charles M. Russell, Albert Bierstadt, and others are displayed in the skillfully restored former city hall. Hours are Monday to Saturday 10:00 a.m. to 5:00 p.m., with weekday closing at 8:00 p.m. in July and August; Sunday noon to 5:00 p.m.

Excellent overnight accommodations are available at Rosewood Inn, a 120-year-old home near the city's center. Fresh fruit and warm bread and cakes are served as what is too-modestly called a Continental breakfast. Rates average about $75 for two people, including breakfast (607-962-3253)

Nearby bed-and-breakfasts include:
Delevan House, 188 Delevan Avenue, Corning, NY (607-962-2347)
"1865" White Birch B&B, 69 East First Street, Corning, NY (607-962-6355)

Bicycle shops
Corning Bike Works, 96 East Market Street, Corning, NY (607-962-7831)
Hillside Bicycles, 75 Bridge Street, Corning, NY (607-936-8124)
Kingsbury's Cyclery, 204 South Main Street, Elmira, NY (607-733-3465)
Little's Bicycles, 1074 South Main Street, Elmira, NY (607-733-3833)
Pedaler's Choice Bikes, 13th and College Avenue, Elmira Heights, NY (607-733-4813)
Qumar, 220 Roe Avenue, Elmira, NY (607-732-0278)

Additional Reading

Adams, Samuel Hopkins. *The Erie Canal.* Random House, 1953.

Andrist, Ralph K. *The Erie Canal.* American Heritage, 1964.

Ballantine, Richard. *Richard's Bicycle Book.* Ballantine Books, 1972.

Clune, Henry W. *The Genesee.* Holt, Rinehart and Winston, 1963.

Ford, Norman. *Keep on Pedaling: The Complete Guide to Adult Bicycling.* The Countryman Press, 1990.

Gurko, Miriam. *The Ladies of Seneca Falls.* Macmillan, 1974.

Jacobs, Stephen W. *Wayne County: The Aesthetic Heritage of a Rural Area.* Publishing Center for Cultural Resources, 1979.

Merrill, Arch. *Slim Fingers Beckon.* American Books-Stratford Press, 1951.

O'Connor, Lois. *A Finger Lakes Odyssey.* North Country Books, 1975.

Palmer, Richard F. *The "Old Line Mail": Stagecoach Days in Upstate New York.* North Country Books, 1977.

Shelgren, Olaf William et al. *Cobblestone Landmarks of New York State.* Syracuse University Press, 1978.

Sloane, Eugene A. *The All New Complete Book of Bicycling.* Simon and Schuster, 1980.

Van Diver, Bradford B. *Upstate New York.* (Geology Field Guide Series) Kendal-Hunt, 1980.

_____. *Roadside Geology of New York.* Mountain Press Publishing Company, 1985.

County Map Sources

Cayuga County Highway Department, 91 York Street, Auburn, NY 13021.

Chemung County Highway Department, Horseheads, NY 14845

Livingston County Highway Department, Conesus, NY 14435

Rochester/Monroe County Convention and Visitors Bureau, Rochester, NY 14604

Onondaga County Highway Department, Syracuse, NY 13202

Ontario County Highway Department, 3907 County Road 46, Canandaigua, NY 14424

Schuyler County Department of Highways, South Decatur Street, Watkins Glen, NY 14891

Seneca County Highway Department, Waterloo, NY 13165

Steuben County Highway Department, Bath, NY 14810

Tompkins County Highway Department, Ithaca, NY 14850

Wayne County Highway Department, Lyons, NY 14489

Yates County Highway Department, P.O. Box 437, Penn Yan, NY 14527

Also from The Countryman Press and Backcountry Publications

The Countryman Press and Backcountry Publications, long known for fine books on travel and outdoor recreation, offer a range of practical and readable manuals.

Bicycling

Keep on Pedaling: The Complete Guide to Adult Bicycling,
   by Norman D. Ford, $12.95

Bicycle Touring Guides

25 Bicycle Tours on Delmarva, $9.95
25 Mountain Bike Tours in Massachusetts:
   From the Connecticut River to the Atlantic, $9.95
25 Bicycle Tours in Eastern Pennsylvania, $8.95
20 Bicycle Tours in the Five Boroughs (NYC), $8.95
25 Bicycle Tours in the Hudson Valley, $9.95
25 Bicycle Tours in Maine, $9.95
30 Bicycle Tours In New Hampshire, $10.95
25 Bicycle Tours in New Jersey, $9.95
20 Bicycle Tours in and around New York City, $7.95
25 Bicycle Tours in Ohio's Western Reserve $11.95
25 Bicycle Tours in Vermont, $9.95
25 Mountain Bike Tours in Vermont, $9.95
25 Bicycle Tours in and around Washington, D.C., $9.95

Other Books for New York residents and visitors:

Canoeing Central New York, $10.95
Discover the South Central Adirondacks, $10.95
Discover the Southwestern Adirondacks, $9.95
Family Resorts of the Northeast, $12.95
Fifty Hikes in the Adirondacks, $12.95
Fifty Hikes in Central Pennsylvania, $10.95
Fifty Hikes in Central New York, $11.95
Fifty Hikes in the Hudson Valley, $12.95
Fifty Hikes in Western New York, $12.95
New England's Special Places, $12.95
Walks & Rambles in Dutchess and Putnam Counties, $10.95
Walks & Rambles in Westchester and Fairfield Counties, $9.95

Our titles are available in bookshops and in many sporting goods stores, or they may be ordered directly from the publisher. When ordering by mail, please add $2.50 per order for shipping and handling. To order or obtain a complete catalog, please write The Countryman Press, Inc., P.O. Box 175, Woodstock, Vermont 05091.